ALSO BY WAYNE WINTERROWD

Annuals for Connoisseurs

The Year at North Hill: Four Seasons in a Vermont Garden (with Joe Eck)

Living Seasonally: The Kitchen and the Table at North Hill (with Joe Eck)

ROSES

ROSES

A Celebration

EDITED BY

WAYNE WINTERROWD

Original paintings by

Pamela Stagg

NORTH POINT PRESS

A DIVISION OF FARRAR, STRAUS AND GIROUX / NEW YORK

North Point Press
A division of Farrar, Straus and Giroux
19 Union Square West, New York 10003

The following selections are included by arrangement with the authors: Rosie Atkins, "*Rosa chinensis* 'Bengal Crimson,'" copyright © 2003 by Rosie Atkins; David Austin, "'Eglantyne,'" copyright © 2003 by David Austin; Peter Beales, "'Great Maiden's Blush,'" copyright © 2003 by Peter Beales; Lloyd Brace, "'Astrid Lindgren,'" copyright © 2003 by Lloyd Brace; Thomas Christopher, "*Rosa chinensis* 'Old Blush,'" copyright © 2003 by Thomas Christopher; Thomas C. Cooper, "'Betty Prior,'" copyright © 2003 by Thomas C. Cooper; Page Dickey, "*Rosa pimpinellifolia* 'Double White,'" copyright © 2003 by Page Dickey; Ken Druse, "*Rosa banksiae* 'Lutea,'" copyright © 2003 by Ken Druse; Rory Dusoir, "*Rosa chinensis* 'Mutabilis,'" copyright © 2003 by Rory Dusoir; Joe Eck and Wayne Winterrowd, "*Rosa glauca*," copyright © 2003 by Joe Eck and Wayne Winterrowd; Joe Eck, "Rose Hips," copyright © 2003 by Joe Eck; Thomas Fischer, "A Trio of Single Roses: 'Mrs Oakley Fisher,' 'Golden Wings,' and 'Darlow's Enigma,'" copyright © 2003 by Thomas Fischer; Jane Garmey, "'New Dawn,'" copyright © 2003 by Jane Garmey; Fergus Garrett, "The Turkish Rose," copyright © 2003 by Fergus Garrett; Mac Griswold, "'Veilchenblau,'" copyright © 2003 by Mac Griswold; Dan Hinkley, "Rosa Rugosa," copyright © 2003 by Dan Hinkley; Jamaica Kincaid, "'Alchymist,'" copyright © 2003 by Jamaica Kincaid; Allen Lacy, "Henry Mitchell's 'Ginny,'" copyright © 2003 by Allen Lacy; Michele and Jean-Claude Lamontagne, "'La Rose de la Paix,'" copyright © 2003 by Michele and Jean-Claude Lamontagne; Christopher Lloyd, "Roses at Great Dixter," copyright © 2003 by Christopher Lloyd; Tovah Martin, "Logee's 'Rosette,'" copyright © 2003 by Tovah Martin; Julie Moir Messervy, "Learning to Like Roses," copyright © 2003 by Julie Moir Messervy; Anthony Noel, "'Variegata di Bologna,'" copyright © 2003 by Anthony Noel; Mirabel Osler, "*Rosa sancta*," copyright © 2003 by Mirabel Osler; Anne Raver, "'Roseraie de l'Haÿ,'" copyright © 2003 by Anne Raver; Graham Stuart Thomas, "'Souvenir de St. Anne's,'" copyright © 2003 by Graham Stuart Thomas; Peter Schneider, "'Corylus,'" copyright © 2003 by Peter Schneider; Lauren Springer, "'Mister Lincoln' and 'Harison's Yellow,'" copyright © 2003 by Lauren Springer; Pamela Stagg, "'Königin von Dänemark,'" copyright © 2003 by Pamela Stagg; David Wheeler, "'Graham Thomas,'" copyright © 2003 by David Wheeler; Wayne Winterrowd, "'Comtesse du Caÿla,'" copyright © 2003 by Wayne Winterrowd; Cynthia Woodyard, "'Kiftsgate,'" copyright © 2003 by Cynthia Woodyard. "'Mme Hardy' and 'Cuisse de Nymphe'" from *Second Nature* by Michael Pollan, copyright © 1991 by Michael Pollan, used by permission of Grove / Atlantic, Inc.

Library of Congress Cataloging-in-Publication Data

Winterrowd, Wayne.
   Roses : a celebration / Wayne Winterrowd.— 1st ed.
     p. cm.
   ISBN 0-86547-661-6 (hc : alk. paper)
   1. Roses. 2. Roses—Varieties. 3. Roses—Pictorial works. 4. Rose culture. I. Title.

SB411.W56 2003
635.9'33734—dc21   2003005765

Designed by Abby Kagan

www.fsgbooks.com

1 3 5 7 9 10 8 6 4 2

For Graham Stuart Thomas

(April 3, 1909–April 16, 2003)

Contents

CONTENTS

viii

ROSES

WAYNE WINTERROWD

Introduction

⌒

T HE ROSE," Alice M. Coates writes in her classic *Garden Shrubs and Their Histories* (1964), "is not a family whose history has been neglected." Beneath her blandness one senses a certain desperation, for the history of the rose has been traced hundreds of times. Learned lectures have been given, conjecture and dispute abound, and new genetic data shift long-established assumptions. Still, what we know of the origins of the rose remains almost as lost to time as are the facts of the Trojan War. To committed rosarians, this tangled history and its confusions are fairly familiar ground. But for those who are new to roses, or who have never thought much beyond their love of them, at least the bare outlines of a long and fascinating history might be traced.

It is certainly the case that other plants—Old World wheat or New World corn, for example—have exercised a far greater influence on humanity than has the rose. But among plants valued for beauty, the rose is unparalleled for its place in myth, symbol, literature, and human affection. As early as the twelfth century B.C., the Persians and the Medes carved representations of the typical, five-petaled single form of the flower as a religious emblem. If we put aside geological evidence, which indicates that roses were flourishing in some form or another long before our species made its appearance, this is our earliest knowledge of the flower. By the tenth century B.C., the Autumn Damask was growing on the island of Samos, where it was considered sacred to Aphrodite. Much later, it was known by the Romans as the Rose of Paestum because it grew in large numbers around the ancient temples of that fourth-century-B.C. city south of modern Naples; one temple, the Temple of Ceres, still stands. The Paestum Rose was celebrated by Virgil because of its ability to produce two flowerings, one in spring and a lesser one in autumn, making it the only repeat-flowering rose known in Europe until the introduction of the China rose in 1781.

The genus *Rosa* is not particularly large. It contains between 100 and 150 species, depending on how finely one wishes to split botanical hairs. But the genus is remarkable for several reasons.

First, its geographic distribution is remarkably broad. Though there are no roses native to South America, Australia, or New Zealand, the dispersal of the genus extends throughout the Northern Hemisphere, from China and Japan through Siberia, down to the Himalayas, and south to the Philippines. It continues from North Africa into Northern Europe, and across the Atlantic to continental North America, down to Mexico. The climatic range of the genus is enormous, stretching from almost arctic conditions to the mildest temperate zones. Such diversity reflects genetic material that is unusually capable of survival and adaptation to a wide (and ever-changing) range of climatic conditions, a heritage that comes to matter hugely in the dispersal of rose species and hybrids throughout the world.

In addition to wide dispersal throughout the Northern Hemisphere, most species within the genus *Rosa* freely intercross with one another when brought into proximity, resulting in many notable natural hybrids. The rose that grew at the temples of Paestum, for example, maintained species identity as *Rosa damascena* var. *bifera* until modern genetic research showed it to be a naturally occurring hybrid between *Rosa gallica* and *R. moschata*. It thus represents the first of thousands of cultivated roses containing the genetic makeup of two or more species or varieties. Another natural cross resulted in the celebrated Bourbon roses early in the nineteenth century. The first of these, 'Rose Edouard,' occurred on an island in the southern Indian Ocean, known once as the Ile de Bourbon and now as Réunion. It was a spontaneous hedgerow mating between the China rose 'Old Blush' and the Autumn Damask, and it was to figure hugely in subsequent rose breeding. Several Bourbons from that period are still much valued in gardens, notably the Empress Josephine's 'Souvenir de la Malmaison,' 'Louise Odier,' 'Mme Isaac Pereire,' and 'Zéphirine Drouhin.'

Until almost the end of the nineteenth century, however, most roses were either true species, the result of crosses by the hazard of proximity, or sports—the spontaneous mutation of flower shape, form, or color. That still left enough to grow, for, though John Gerard recorded only fourteen roses in his *Herball* (1597), the botanist John Parkinson—always the better gardener—writing in 1629, included twenty-four in his. Even with so relatively small a number, he could write that "the great variety of roses . . . is much to be admired." He little knew.

By 1799, Mary Lawrance was able to publish *A Collection of Roses from Nature*, really the first of the great rose picture books, with ninety hand-colored etchings, and by the first decade of the nineteenth century, the Empress Josephine had accumulated so large a collection at Malmaison that she encouraged Pierre Joseph Redouté in the publication of his folio volumes, four in number, containing 170 plates. The Empress died in 1814, and so she never saw the publication of Redouté's work, which began in 1817 and continued to 1824. Still, his four folios represent perhaps the greatest work on roses ever published, and mark the beginning of the keen enthusiasm that has continued to our time.

It is important to realize, however, that scientific knowledge of the mechanics of breeding was not well established until Gregor Mendel undertook his work on heredity in the 1860s, after which the principles of hybridization through human intervention began to be understood. The Dutch had made a frenzy of crosses and selections in the seventeenth century, but it was not until around 1890 that a true explosion of rose varieties occurred, scarcely abating to the present day, and producing plants of such genetic complexity that the mind reels. Any hybrid bred before the end of the nineteenth century would contain the genes of several species. *Rosa centifolia*, for example, developed in Holland and known as Rose des Peintres because of its presence in so many seventeenth-

century Dutch floral paintings, displays the genetic material of *Rosa gallica,
R. phoenicia, R. moschata, R. canina,* and *R. × damascena.* But when modern cytologists examine a recent hybrid—'Tropicana,' say, or 'Sterling Silver'—they may find evidence of a dozen species or more, and countless hybrids among them, reflecting what Hugh Johnson in *The Principles of Gardening* (1979) calls "a cocktail of inextricable complexity."

That brings us to the third remarkable fact about the genus *Rosa.* No other in the entire botanical kingdom reflects so long, so persistent, and so devoted an intervention by the hand of man. Written records of the cultivation of roses extend back more than five thousand years from the present, but there is ample though unwritten evidence of an even longer history, particularly in China and the ancient Middle East. One might suppose that the extraordinary beauty of the rose accounts for its elevation above all other flowers. However, the deliberate cultivation of flowering plants for their beauty appears to be only a periodic occurrence in Western history until the classical Roman period, when gardening as we in the West understand it began. (In China it is of older date, and the China roses—which would prove so important in nineteenth-century breeding for their characteristic of repeat blooming—already represented a complex but unrecorded series of crossings, intercrossings, and selections by the time of their arrival in Holland and England in the late eighteenth century.) In fact, no other plant of pronounced flower beauty was cultivated through the early Middle Ages, with the possible exception of the lily, the status of which was assured in monastery gardens because of its iconographic association with the Virgin Mary.

Roses, however, along with fruits and herbs, are among those few plants that possess both aesthetic and economic importance. It is a peculiarity of some roses, most particularly *Rosa gallica* var. *officinalis,* the Apothecary's Rose, that the fragrance of their petals endures long after they are dried, and a belief in the therapeutic properties of this fragrance exists from earliest human history down to the present time. The late Middle Ages practiced its own version of aromatherapy, equating pungency with efficaciousness in the treatment of disease. So the strong fragrance of some rose petals when harvested and dried was judged both healthful and delightful—no dichotomy in a world where the malodorousness of poor sanitation and the occurrence of ill health went hand in hand. Huge numbers of *R. gallica officinalis* plants were cultivated from the thirteenth to the nineteenth centuries around the city of Provins, southeast of Paris, and their petals were harvested and processed into pastes, oils, and unguents, producing a veritable pharmacopeia of remedies for all human surface ailments, including damaged skin, ulcers, wounds, amputations, and eye injury and disease.

An awareness of the rose as a medicinal plant was most likely brought home by the first Crusaders from North Africa and the Middle East, where knowledge of the therapeutic, culinary, and olfactory benefits of rose petals had been passed down from the ancient classical period. Without fixatives or complex chemical manipulation, few flowers lend themselves so well to preserving. Even before the Middle Ages, in Turkey and the Middle East, the process by which certain roses could be made into conserves, powders, or waters was well understood, resulting in products that were healthful in themselves and could also be used to flavor sweets and prepared dishes. The cream-filled pastries heavily scented with rose water that are sold in Greece and Sicily, and some sections of New York City, are a remnant of this practice. In Turkey, the scent is included in many dishes, both sweet and savory, to this day.

The ruggedness of the rose has also had something to do with its survival through history, including some of the darkest periods of the Middle Ages. To begin with, roses are shrubs, even though in some cases (such as *Rosa filipes* and its famous selection, 'Kiftsgate') they may make use of their wickedly hooked thorns to throw growth upward into any support, reaching heights of fifty feet or more. Their shrubby, deep-rooted character gives them an advantage over annuals, bulbs, or herbaceous plants, because they can withstand years of neglect in rough meadows, abandoned gardens, or other untended places. But roses also sprout suckers, new growth originating from below ground. In this way, most roses form wide thickets that expand annually from the mother plant, producing a dense shade that eliminates competitors.

Perhaps more than any other, this characteristic has suited roses wonderfully well, resulting in the spread of rose species and naturally occurring hybrids from ancient times to the present, wherever gardening has been practiced. Experienced gardeners, confronted with a rose on its own roots that they want for their garden, will say, "Just give me a bit of root." They will cut off the top of the sucker, down to perhaps two inches, but preserve carefully the blackened, swollen bit between where the shoot grew above ground and its juncture to the mother plant, since there the life is. Roses travel well, and thousands of bits have thus been dug from ancient cities, ancestral houses, or family graveyards, protected from desiccation by nothing more than a little moist straw or cloth, and planted to grow again. Roses were transported in this way first across the ancient world, then on the packhorses of the Crusaders, later on ships bringing exotic species from China and the New World into Europe, and eventually on wagon trains that distributed old species and varieties throughout North America.

But roses have many other ways of reproducing than through the stolons that most of them naturally form. Cuttings also strike readily, and when properly protected can be transported long distances. More than one bundle of a choice species or family heirloom has crossed continents and oceans in damp straw, in oiled paper, in a plastic bag, or—as Vita Sackville-West once improvised when traveling in North Africa—stuck into a large potato. The great Southern garden writer Elizabeth Lawrence once noticed a particularly beautiful rose in a garden and asked its owner the name. "It is the Annasent rose," he replied. "We call it that because Anna sent it." In what form Miss Lawrence did not record, though it might have come as a rooted bit or a cutting and still survived after long travel.

Roses also set seed, which is abundantly produced in hips, an antique English word designating the fruit of the plant and sometimes, in old-fashioned texts, still written "heps." Though the seed is generally fertile, it is often extremely acidic, and therefore one of the most concentrated sources of vitamin C known. It will eventually be eaten by hungry birds when winter frosts have taken out the sourness, and then be widely dispersed. Glutinous hairs on the seeds of most roses stick to a bird's beak and can only be removed by being rubbed off on small twigs or branches, which assures an even wider dispersal than if all the seed passed through the bird's digestive system and was expelled in one place. If the rose is a species, such as the beach rose, *Rosa rugosa*, or the dreaded pasture rose, *R. multiflora*, sprouted seed will be true to its parent, producing either an identical copy or some variant encoded within its genetic makeup. An amble in late June or early July along the beach anywhere on Cape Cod or parts of the Maine coast, where the Asian species *Rosa rugosa* is widely naturalized, will thus reveal several shades of single pink roses, and some that are white, with—if one is very lucky—even a rare double-flowered form. An examination of thickets of *R. multiflora* will also occasionally reveal a completely thornless plant, which rose growers treasure as grafting stock for its ease of handling, and which gardeners who like the appearance and strong scent of *R. multiflora* collect for growing on arbors or to run up into trees.

But if the rose is a hybrid, the result of pollenization by some random bee, the wind, or human agency, a new rose may occur—one that may be very desirable. Hybridists, both professional and amateur, make thousands of crosses a year, as does Nature itself, and no one can say how many splendid roses have been ignored or discarded because of fashion, or because the hybridizer was set on a clearer scarlet, a finer bud, or a hardier plant, or simply because no one stumbled upon them. Nevertheless, the number of rose varieties now in existence runs to many thousands, and, as Peter Schneider points out in his essay for this book, "Crossing any modern rose with any other modern rose [may] produce one of seventeen million different possible results." Though a few desirable roses are either naturally occurring hybrids or sports, most are raised from seed. Their numbers increase yearly, and are apt to do so as long as the fashions of the moment elevate one look, one color, one bud or flower formation over others. We may truly, then, echo Browning's much-quoted line and say that, for much of human history, "It is roses, roses all the way."

But the capacity to survive—by cutting, stolon, seed, climatic adaptability, or otherwise—though obviously important to any individual plant genus, may still not be of much value to humanity. Any persistent weed may possess as many tricks as does the rose, just to get by. "What is this ROSE," Graham Thomas asks in his great *Rose Book* (1994), "that enslaves gardeners? . . . Why, in short, does everyone love a rose, and what does it offer that other flowers lack?" His reply to the question is scent. That might have served as a first answer, many centuries back, and serves still to many. But other flowers may smell as sweet. Consider the lily, whose scent is generally rich, and whose species are as numerous. Or the rhododendron, which may be had in a huge number of colors and forms, many possessing a fine fragrance of their own. And today many hybrids and modern teas either have a weak scent or are wholly lacking in that wonderful attribute, yet are still valued.

The qualities we have so far detailed—ruggedness, ease of transport, genetic diversity, susceptibility to manipulation by the hand of man, adaptability to a wide range of climatic conditions, economic use—eke out an answer to some degree. There is also, of course, the innate charm of the rose, whether as a pure, single flower of five petals or a much-doubled and -quartered opulent cup such as 'Mme Hardy' or 'Cuisse de Nymphe,' or even the perfect, high-centered bud of the florist's hybrid tea. Pretty flowers, all. But we must still look a little further.

No flower has achieved anything near the prominence of the rose in the human imagination—not as a real flower, but as an idea. From those twelfth-century Persian carvings onward, it was employed as a religious symbol. In earliest Greek religious history, it was associated with Aphrodite, and came to represent youthful purity. Later, to the Romans, it was the flower of Venus, and also of Bacchus, a symbol for luxury and indulgence, making up the chaplet worn by banqueters at feasts, their couches scattered with its petals. In the Middle Ages, the white rose became associated with the purity of the Virgin Mary, and, by extension, the red rose with Christ's Passion. By the Renaissance, the rose had again been associated with the beauties and pleasures of the world, showering Botticelli's newborn Venus with its petals, and showing up in the baroque and even classical periods as the bouquet clasped by a leering Bacchus, or draping the chaste bosom of Houdon's portrait bust of the Comtesse du Caÿla. Seventeenth-century Dutch still-life painters saw in the rose, particularly the opulent centifolias, the very emblem of both the joys of life and its inevitable end. The rose then became the symbol of two warring English noble houses, the Yorks (red) and the Lancasters (white), and the name of an internecine war between them, which ended with the marriage of Henry of Lancaster, later Henry VII, to Elizabeth of York. To the Victorians, who could attach symbolic meaning to anything, roses were rich in significance, and so, in the Language of Flowers, red roses conveyed fidelity, a single yellow bloom jealousy, and endlessly on. The modern florist industry has grown rich on Valentine's Day with the sale of red roses, a bunched dozen of which is as obligatory a romantic pledge as a heart-shaped box of chocolates.

The interesting thing about human symbols is that they take on a life of their own, gaining strength with each expression, and sometimes becoming far distant from, or at least something other than, the thing they originally represented. The stylized acanthus leaves on Corinthian columns, for example, are instantly familiar to us, having been employed as architectural decoration for more than three thousand years, though few would recognize in them the Mediterranean woodland plant on which they were originally modeled. Similarly, by always seeming to be something more than itself, the rose has become far more than it was, or, indeed, in the minds of all but gardeners, more than it is. It has entered the English language in myriad and surprising ways. Michael Pollan, in his chapter on roses in *Second Nature* (1991), assembles this litany.

> . . . the War of the Roses . . . the crown of thorns . . . *rosy-fingered dawn . . .* sub rosa . . . *Rose is a rose is a rose* . . . the rosary . . . the Rosicrucians . . . *The Romance of the Rose* . . . the Rose Bowl . . . the bed of roses . . . *by any other name would smell as sweet* . . . Dante's yellow rose of Paradise . . . *when the fire and the rose are one* . . . the run for the roses . . . *toward the door we never opened / Into the rose garden* . . . through rose-colored glasses . . . Rosebud . . . Tennyson's *white rose of virginity* . . .

He concludes by noting that the rose is a "symbol, it almost seems, of symbols."

To the writers assembled in this book, individual roses have also meant something other than, or more than, themselves. Many have valued a single rose, not only for what beauty it possesses, but also for how it came to matter to them. Anyone who cares for flowers will know that any flower, if it is remembered at all, can be a hook on which to hang both memory and desire, but the rose seems better for that than any other. Hence this book, which is made up of essays not so much about roses as about personal memories of them. Voices vary from essay to essay. Perspectives vary, and the roses themselves vary—though there is conversation among them, an echoing of attitudes, preferences, and the prejudices that are—like it or not—the mother of taste. At bottom, these essays have this in common: the conviction that almost anything deeply loved or valued, even a single rose, catches up the strands of history and memory—of how something counted in childhood or at some other point in our lives because of where we happened to be or what we were making or whom we were with, and how we felt at that moment.

WAYNE
WINTERROWD

Rosa 'Great Maiden's Blush'

PETER BEALES

'Great Maiden's Blush'

⤳

I HAVE ACCEPTED an impossible charge—to write an essay on "my favorite rose." I do not have such a thing. My favorite rose is a rose, and my favorite roses are roses, so how can I pretend otherwise? Easy, indulge in a little favoritism.

"Favoritism" is defined in my dictionary as "the unfair favoring of one over others," so, in this context, my pet rose has always been that temperamental, once-flowering, wet-weather-hating, but stunningly beautiful 'Maiden's Blush.' It is a member of the *alba* family of roses, and it has come down to us from the very distant past, avoiding extinction, the fate of so many of the old roses, by its will to live to a great old age even in some of the most hostile of environments, surviving on the captivating charm of its delicate pink, full-face flowers, and, perhaps above all, its exquisite perfume.

I first fell in love with 'Maiden's Blush' as a child. I have a vivid and cherished memory of my first introduction to it by my grandfather when I was about four years old. Although Grandfather was a vegetable grower, it being wartime then, he loved to share his enjoyment of gardening with me. His rose—the name of which he did not know—was the only rose in his garden, and no one else but we two could touch it. Or so I thought. Certainly no blooms were ever cut from the bush to be taken indoors—a tradition upheld to this day, for the same plant, which I came to know so well all those years ago, is still thriving under my mother's care in the garden of our family home in North Norfolk.

I had no inkling, all those years ago, that I would one day make my living from roses. But in the mid-1960s, when I started my rose-growing business, I cut the budding eyes for the propagation of my first crop of 'Great Maiden's Blush' from that old bush that had become known by my family as "Granddad's rose." It gives me great pleasure to know that each plant my rose nursery now distributes around the world came from stock of the first rose I ever knew.

As most devotees of roses will know, there are two forms of 'Maiden's Blush,' known respectively as 'Great' and 'Small,' definitions that refer specifically to stature. The former, as the name suggests, is quite capable of growing up to a height of ten or fifteen feet. The latter seldom attains a height of more than four feet. As far as I can tell, there is little or no difference in the size of their respective flowers. There is, however, sometimes a considerable variation in the depth of color of the flowers in both forms, but this seems to be a phenomenon related to either soil or climate, or possibly both. The two forms are equally resistant to disease, and both are extremely shade-tolerant, therefore having many uses as garden plants. Although the 'Great' form is still essentially a large shrub rose, from time to time I like to use it as a climber, allowing it to thread its way up into the branches of a small tree. When grown this way, it can be most rewarding, and its tolerance of shade gives it an advantage over most other climbing roses of similar coloring, for it never seems to sulk amongst dense foliage. It just gets on with life. It will even grow happily if planted on the north side of conifer trees, where it will filter its branches through to produce flowers on the brighter, south side.

In their different capacities, both the 'Great' and the 'Small' forms of 'Maiden's Blush' are very good mixers when used in association with other shrubs or perennials, their leaden-green leaves combining well, in particular, with plants having maroon or plum-colored foliage. They will also make good hedges if tended properly. The 'Great' form is best pruned judiciously from time to time to make an informal hedgerow. The 'Small' form has a naturally tidier habit, and therefore makes an ideal upright-growing but bushy hedge. The best way to achieve this effect is to reduce the current year's flowering shoots to half their length in the earlier years of growth, a task that should be done immediately after the plants have finished flowering each summer. This helps to encourage density of growth in the formative years. Later, from about the third or fourth year onward, the only pruning necessary to keep the hedge in shape is to remove all the spent blossoms with shears.

The longevity of 'Maiden's Blush' is borne out by the fact that it is far and away the most common of all the roses that are sent to me each year for identification. More often than not, these requests are accompanied by delightful little nostalgic stories, as, for example: "My grandma knew this rose as a child, and her mother told her that the bush from which I send this example came from a plant which she, too, recalled from her youth." A less common reason for inquiry—though still frequent enough—is the sudden appearance of this rose in a part of the garden where no rose has ever before been seen growing. Such a surprising emergence is usually the result of the rhizomelike roots of 'Maiden's Blush,' which, having been hindered from sprouting for one reason or another (usually because of the constant cultivation of a border or the regular cutting of a lawn), suddenly reappear above ground. Such is the will of this rose to live that a new plant can emerge many years after its parent has disappeared, and many yards from its original position.

As with other members of the *alba* family, one of the most endearing attributes of 'Maiden's Blush' is its fragrance, which I have referred to as exquisite. In addition of course to its good looks, this characteristic is what most singles it out for my favoritism. I look forward to its blooming with relish each year as winter passes and summer approaches. That it will not display its flowers again after the first flush is singularly unimportant to me. Indeed, it is the very transience of these flowers that endears "Maiden's Blush' to me so much. On occasions when it may produce only one perfect bloom each summer, which is sometimes the case in our English climate, such is its loveliness that I am contented for the whole year to come.

Rosa 'Souvenir de St. Anne's'

GRAHAM STUART THOMAS

'Souvenir de St. Anne's'

ST. ANNE'S PARK, near Dublin, was the home of Lady Ardilaun, who had a good garden in the earlier part of the twentieth century. Among the roses she grew was 'Souvenir de la Malmaison,' and in her garden this famous, very double blush-pink rose produced a sport with very few petals. It was essentially a semi-double, quite lovely in its simplicity. She gave cuttings of it to Lady Moore, a famous gardener in her own right and the wife of Sir Frederick Moore, for many years the Keeper of the Glasnevin Botanic Garden, near Dublin. With her gift, Lady Ardilaun expressed to Lady Moore the wish that she should not give away that rose again. That is a request which is always to be respected, and Lady Moore grew it for many years at Willbrook House, Rathfarnham, Dublin, taking both satisfaction in its growth and pleasure in the appearance of its flower. After Lady Ardilaun's death, Lady Moore gave propagating material to me, and I introduced it in due course as 'Souvenir de St. Anne's.' This name was Lady Moore's suggestion, as a way of commemorating the garden of her old friend. St. Anne's itself is now a public park, and, appropriately, a bed of this rose is in full evidence there.

But let us go back a bit further. The parent of 'Souvenir de St. Anne's,' 'Souvenir de la Malmaison,' was raised by Jean Béluze at Lyon in 1843. (Only two roses are recorded as having been raised by him, this one and 'Gloire d'Orient,' a deep red which I have never seen.) The Empress Josephine, who created the first large collection of roses at her château at Malmaison, near Paris, died in 1814, and so, quite contrary to popular belief, she never grew this rose. It was named in her honor by the Grand Duke of Russia, who had obtained a plant for the Imperial Garden at St. Petersburg. Béluze recorded that 'Souvenir de la Malmaison' was a cross between 'Mme Desprez' and an unspecified tea rose. Since its appearance, it has never been out of cultivation, though at one time it acquired another name, 'Queen of Beauty and Fragrance.'

'Souvenir de la Malmaison' makes a sturdy, freely branching shrub that in my garden is out of flower only for the occasional odd week between mid-June and the autumn. It bears large, very double flowers with masses of overlapping petals of a pale creamy pink. It has some scent, verging toward the tea fragrance, but I have never found it free enough in this respect to justify the last part of the second name it acquired. A climbing sport originated in 1893, and though it is a strong grower, it is by no means as freely reblooming as its parent.

Now we may come to the particular value of 'Souvenir de St. Anne's.' It is known that the Bourbon roses have in their inheritance not only the old French once-flowering roses but also a tincture of *Rosa moschata*, the musk rose. That species has close relatives all through the Northern Hemisphere, such as *R. setigera* (North America), *R. wichuraiana*, and *R. multiflora* (Japan), and many lesser-known but vigorous climbers, all with single white flowers, native to western China and other parts of East Asia. They share two very marked botanical characteristics which distinguish them from all other species in the genus *Rosa*. Their styles (stigmas) do not stand free but, rather, are united into a single column, and their scent is in their stamens, not their petals.

It is important to understand all this, because 'Souvenir de St. Anne's,' being nearly single, possesses prominent stamens, and so bears a sweet and lovely scent reminiscent of cloves, whereas 'Souvenir de la Malmaison,' being quite double, possesses a much slighter scent, if, indeed, one can discern any at all.

From this knot of 'Souvenir de la Malmaison' and 'Souvenir de St. Anne's,' one may trace the threads of this history still further. For, according to Dr. C. C. Hurst, an eminent geneticist of the last century, the Bourbon roses, of which 'Souvenir de la Malmaison' is one, were initially the result of crosses between the Autumn Damask and 'Parson's Pink China.' The Autumn Damask was itself of ancient European origin, a hybrid with the *gallica* rose, the musk rose, and *Rosa fedtschenkoana* from Turkestan in its parentage. 'Parson's Pink China,' on the other hand, was an ancient Chinese hybrid that united *R. chinensis* with *R. gigantea*. The result of that crossing was a repeat-flowering rose, and as the two last were also repeat-flowering, many of the resulting progeny possessed this desirable characteristic to one degree or another. 'Souvenir de St. Anne's' is an example of the luckier ones; it is seldom out of flower in my garden except in the coldest weather.

Having investigated the parentage of 'Souvenir de St. Anne's,' I feel I must add a note on another of the distinguished offspring of 'Souvenir de la Malmaison,' the famous old 'Gloire de Dijon.' It dates from 1853, and is the direct result of crossing the Malmaison rose with an unspecified but evidently vigorous tea. In my *Rose Book*, I write, "With its many assets it was indeed an epoch-making rose, at a time when yellow roses were tender, or drooping, or pale." For many decades it was the most famous yellow climbing rose, with a wonderful scent. It has the further distinction of having been the favorite rose of the Reverend Dean Reynolds-Hole, first president of the National Rose Society, and it was made famous by his writings. It is still well worth growing.

To sum up, I fear I would not give high marks to 'Climbing Souvenir de la Malmaison.' It is too long out of flower in summer, though one must confess that its autumn blooms can often be very good. On the other hand, 'La Malmaison' itself is a superlative performer from early summer until late fall, a characteristic inherited by its sport, 'Souvenir de St. Anne's.' They are both strong and bushy, with good foliage, and they do not disappoint when grown with shrubs and other plants of all kinds. Their delicate pink petals—palest in 'St. Anne's'—consort well with the crimson sepals and purple skirts of hardy fuchsias such as *Fuchsia magellanica* and its many forms, the slender stems and foliage of which will provide a pleasing contrast with the roses which are close to nearly the same height.

How blessed we are with these two fine roses that provide color for almost half the year!

GRAHAM
STUART
THOMAS

24

Rosa 'Alchymist'

JAMAICA KINCAID

'Alchymist'

Is this a good thing for me to be doing, actually putting into writing the idea that I have a favorite rose? Do I have a favorite rose? Does anybody? How can anybody like one rose above all others? There are so many roses to begin with, and then there are even more. When people meet roses, they fall in love with them so much that a whole process of tampering is set in motion. And yet there is one rose I love and would be very sorry not to have growing in my garden.

My favorite rose, then, is 'Alchymist.' Its provenance is 'Golden Glow' and an unspecified *R. eglanteria* hybrid. It came into my life in this way: I was at the most feeble and ignorant stage of my gardening life—I was at the beginning. The house I live in now was new to me. It had some old flower beds, planted with peonies (big red-maroon things), roses (small pink fragrant blossoms that came at once in early June and that was that), and some daylilies (*Hemerocallis fulva*). Without hesitating, I began to move some things here, other things there, and when I grew tired of that, I dug up and threw away the rest. How I regret that now, the throwing-away part. Especially I regret throwing away all those roses.

But in those days, I approached the garden with great certainty—not confidence, just certainty—that everything I did and thought was so clearly the right thing to do. I certainly did not like flowers that bloomed fleetingly, and I would not grow them.

In those days, I made many trips each day to places where garden things could be purchased. I would find that I needed things to make the soil more sweet and things to make the soil more sour; something that would make a plant produce more leaves and something that would make it bear more fruit. I was so much at the store getting things to make a plant do what a plant will do, I often forgot that a plant knew how to do anything at all by itself. I never went to the garden store to buy plants; I bought most of my plants through the mail. I went to the garden store to buy things that are meant to support plants.

But, of course, one of the unfortunate things about gardening is how it puts you in an acquisitive mood. So it was that on one of those many trips to the garden store I bought something that I had not gone to the garden store to buy in the first place. I saw two rosebushes in five-gallon pots, and, without knowing what kind of rosebushes they were, I bought them. They cost me almost ten dollars each.

One of the roses turned out to be a 'Henry Kelsey' (a nice red rose that seems to enjoy a fair amount of mistreatment, which it gets from me both on purpose and accidentally), and the other was the now much-loved and treasured 'Alchymist.' I planted them and replanted them a few times before I was satisfied that I had gotten rose planting right. The year after, 'Henry Kelsey' bloomed but 'Alchymist' did not.

That first year, when 'Alchymist' did not bloom, I was on the verge of uprooting it and placing it in that netherworld of plants tossed out. But I saved the rose and the tag that came with it, a little piece of stiff paper on which appeared the words "*R. Alchymist*," and next to that a picture of a peach-colored, open-faced flower, my rose. Over the next couple of years, many things happened. I found that I had started to make a garden without meaning to do so, for one thing. I thought I was just putting plants in the ground in a way that pleased me, but almost behind my own back, certainly without any true purpose, I was making a garden. All that time, while the 'Alchymist' just sat there, throwing out ten-foot-long cane after ten-foot-long cane, making the act of growing seem a form of languishing, I got all sorts of ideas about the garden, and they were not limited to shady and sunny, hardy and tender. I came to know the garden as the place where conquest becomes a beautiful distraction. The rose all by itself is a splendid example: some of them come to us from someplace Alexander the Great passed through, some of them come to us through the travels of a priest, and so forth.

I had just begun to make my way in the garden, but was quite full of myself and my little observations, and not at all afraid to declare them. This made many gardeners I knew who had been laboring for many years resentful. One day I was having a conversation with a gardener I knew and admired for her delphiniums. When I told her of the ease I had growing them, she told me the error I had been making that led to this ease. I was properly chastened, but at parting, perhaps feeling I needed a little more chastisement, I told her that I had planted the rose 'Alchymist' and how worried I was about it, for it had never bloomed. My friend told me that of course this rose would never bloom for me, it was not meant for my climate, too tender, my cold winters would kill the old canes. Didn't I know that 'Alchymist' blooms on old canes? How sad it was that I did not know more about the things I had planted in my garden, how sad it was that I did not know more about the garden in general, how lucky I was to know someone who knew more about the garden than I did.

Feeling properly humbled, I went home and looked at my rose. I was sad. Implied in my friend's sturdy and authoritative advice was the notion that I should give up the idea of cultivating this particular rose altogether; that I should find another rose (the suggestion was 'Roseraie de l'Haÿ) that would suit the cold southern-Vermont climate in which I live. But I have never liked people telling me what to do. When I am told what to do, I do its opposite, even when what I am told to do is the right thing to do.

Three years after I planted the 'Alchymist,' it bloomed. When I first detected its buds, I thought it was coming down with an illness I had not yet read about, so accustomed had I become to seeing canes of leaves and thorns. As the buds grew bigger, I was sure my plant was dying. In hours (twenty-four to thirty-six) they went from bud to flower—yellow, peach, or pink, depending on how my eye perceived those colors or what light they were seen in.

This difficult distinction, between pure perception and what influences my perception, captures the distinct nature of this rose, for 'Alchymist' is never a model of stability. It will sometimes seem to go from yellow to peach to pink, or start out pink and go to yellow and then peach. It starts out as if it will be the usual tea rose, and then it develops into the fullest quartered rose I have ever seen. Every description of it I have read says it is scented, even highly scented. Mine have no scent at all. I have five plants growing in different parts of the garden, each of them bought from a different place, and they all have the same characteristic unpredictability and no fragrance at all. The absence of fragrance is strong.

That my favorite rose is one that I am not supposed to be able to grow and that by its nature is not predictable does not surprise me. I take it as a given that all things worth loving are difficult, hard to pin down, and changeable, all the while being true to themselves. The 'Alchymist' can do whatever it wants, but it remains a rose, the rose that I love.

Rosa 'Roseraie de l'Haÿ'

ANNE RAVER

'Roseraie de l'Haÿ'

I HAVE LOST my favorite *Rosa rugosa*, 'Roseraie de l'Haÿ.' I kept meaning to dig it up when I got back to Red Hook, my old neighborhood in Brooklyn, where great ships used to steam up the Buttermilk Channel, bearing raw sugar, coffee, and cocoa to New York's bustling port. Those days are long gone now, and the abandoned docks have sprouted mugwort and ailanthus. In recent years, artists and gardeners, drawn to the light and the sea, have fixed up the old row houses, weathered burglaries and muggings, witnessed a few shootouts on the main drag, and planted gardens in the backyards.

*Rugosa*s do well on those windy shores. I planted a handful of them with my neighbors one fall, on the edge of a rocky outcropping that reached into the rushing water where the Hudson and East Rivers meet to pour into the Buttermilk Channel. We would gather there at sunset, to watch the sky turn pink and coral behind the Statue of Liberty, and the skyscrapers to the north, on Manhattan, turn into millions of twinkling lights.

I would say to myself, "This is a fine place to live. Buy a fixer-upper and settle down." But then my childhood memories of Maryland's rolling hills would float into my mind, and a siren voice would sing, "Remember how sweet the springs are, how long the falls. The stone walls of the family's old barnyard would make a perfect garden." So I wouldn't go looking in Red Hook. Or if I did, I'd look for a house too perfect to find.

It was a chilly day when we put in the roses—just spindly runners dug from a sprawling *rugosa* in a nearby yard—and we weren't too careful about it. We used pickaxes to dig holes in the sandy crevices between the rocks, tossing in a shovelful of compost with each scrubby stick.

To my amazement, they soon took root, and sprouted leaves in the spring. By summer, the vigorous little bushes were sporting a few velvety deep-pink flowers. I would lean over and take a deep breath of that mix of cloves and salt—and be transported back to the dunes of Nantucket, where I first fell in love with the beach roses that covered the banks of an old fishing village called Siasconset, and a young writer who lived there. I never knew, until years later, long after that man and I had married and divorced—because we didn't know what it takes to love—that these velvet roses had not been born on the beach.

"*Rosa rugosa*s are native to Japan and northeastern Asia," Graham Stuart Thomas told me rather sternly one morning, as we stood in the cold rain at Montisfont Abbey in Stockbridge, England. Sternly, because the legendary English gardener was taking me on a tour of the walled garden where he had planted more than 350 varieties of roses—many of which he had personally saved from oblivion—and if he had gone to all that trouble, at least I could have done my homework. To make it worse, I was having trouble remembering the Latin names of the columnar junipers, the varieties of clematis winding up the old apple trees, the yellow foxgloves and white lilies he had so carefully chosen to complement his roses. And then this rain! Mr. Thomas looked near tears as he stood over the bashed white blossoms of his dear 'Mme Hardy,' a damask rose that looked, in the downpour, like crumpled wet tissues. All I wanted was to find a pub where I could warm my frozen fingers around a cup of strong English tea laced with whiskey, but Mr. Thomas plunged on, despite his eighty-eight years, to point out *Rosa gallica*, the dainty pink single from Southern Europe, and 'Belle de Crécy,' a fragrant *gallica* whose petals are a mix of cerise, violet, and lilac-gray, and on and on until I stopped him in front of a mass of roses with sturdy green leaves and violet-colored flowers that smelled like cloves. This rose was standing up to the rain like a sailor embracing a gale.

"What's this purple rose?" I asked, burying my nose in the petals, which swirled around creamy stamens. The fragrance, even in that rain, took me straight back to Nantucket.

"It's not purple, it's MUR-rey," Mr. Thomas said. Really, this American didn't know anything. " 'MUR-rey' is the word for that shade of crimson-purple, like mulberries." The rose itself, he said, was 'Roseraie de l'Haÿ,' propagated in 1901 by Jules Gravereaux, who apparently crossed a sport of some *rugosa* with another rose, and named it after the garden he created near Paris. "MUR-rey," I dutifully repeated through clenched teeth, trying to look focused. When I started to shake uncontrollably, Mr. Thomas gave me a piercing look and suggested, finally, that we retire to a pub.

After I returned to New York, I began to look for 'Roseraie de l'Haÿ' whenever I came across a good nursery. I could have ordered it through the mail, I knew, but I didn't want it to arrive in a box, a couple of sticks with a few rumpled leaves. I wanted to see those murrey petals again, and inhale their enchanting scent. I found my rose in a little nursery on Long Island's sandy, salty North Fork. The baby shrub's grass-green leaves and velvety buds were bristling out of a one-gallon plastic pot, like a puppy begging for a home. I took it back to the roof garden in Brooklyn Heights, where I then lived, and planted it, five flights up, among the moonflower vines that liked to climb over the tarpapered smokestack.

I loved that garden, with its field of pots, its neighboring water towers, and its view of the clock tower on top of the Watchtower building, so you knew exactly what time the sun set, or the cars jammed up on the Manhattan Bridge. My friends and I were sublimely above it all, as we wolfed down fresh pesto and smelled the moonflowers—and 'Roseraie de l'Haÿ'—mingling with the diesel fumes. When I moved to Red Hook, I took my roses with me, prying their roots from the cedar planters and wrapping them in damp newspaper for their ten-minute ride down Court Street, which used to lead straight to the docks. Now you go under the Brooklyn-Queens Expressway, dog-leg around a housing project, soccer fields, and a run-down public pool, and voilà, you're in the old sailors' village.

I was renting the third floor of an old brick house, so I had no garden, and had to farm my plants out to friends, who promised them back as soon as I got a place of my own. There was an old carriage house I had my eye on that reminded me of a barn.

Memory is a funny thing. I could swear that 'Roseraie' went to a friend in Red Hook who had long been a homeowner herself. I planted it alongside 'Russell's Cottage,' an old shrub rose I'd grown from cuttings taken one June afternoon from a New Jersey cemetery. I remember tucking both of them against the southwest corner of her house, and trying hard to charm her first-floor tenant, who was not thrilled to share any of his garden with a stranger. But when the roses bloomed the next June, no one minded, and as the years went by, I just left them there, visiting now and then to enjoy their blooms, and a beer and conversation with my friend.

Now I've finally answered the siren's call. I've moved back to the old family farm in Maryland. I'm building a house in the barn, turning one of the haylofts into a SoHo-like loft full of windows that face south, over the fields. I've even found someone to share all this with, and now, I hope, I know how to love. So this spring I thought I was ready to plant my roses. I watched the light travel over the stone foundation of an old chicken house my grandfather built near the barn about a century ago. Its three walls, snuggled against the bank of a hill yet open to the sun, seemed perfect for a handful of shrubs and climbers, maybe a few clematis and lilies, even some yellow foxglove, in honor of Mr. Thomas.

I could picture 'Roseraie de l'Haÿ' sprawling in a great hedge along the top of the bank. So I went back to Red Hook in May, when the old yards are tumbling with roses, thinking I could take a few cuttings of my favorite rose, or dig up some runners. I couldn't dig up the whole plant. It would be too crass after all those years, like a mother who gives away her baby and then wants her little girl back.

I showed up at my friend's house, shovel in hand, clippers in my back pocket, and we went out to the backyard. 'Russell's Cottage' was there, now a sprawling bush laden with loose purple-red flowers swirled with white. But no one could remember 'Roseraie de l'Haÿ.'

"You know, the purple-red one"—I didn't say "MUR-rey"—"that smells like cloves." My friend shook her head. Too many tenants had come and gone, changing the garden from corn and tomatoes to fiery annuals, to grapevines and perennials. I scouted out all the other roses. Not a trace of 'Roseraie de l'Haÿ.'

"Maybe I planted it on Dikeman Street," I said, meaning my old landlord's backyard, but that house, too, had changed hands. "Or did I take it to Maine?" I'd taken more than a few roses out to an island off the coast, where my sister and her husband have a cottage.

I had gardened in my own mind for so long, the real plants had found homes of their own.

I've collected other roses these past few years—'Gertrude Jekyll,' *Rosa mundi*, the yellow one named 'Graham Thomas'—and every May, they bloom in a jumble of yellows, pinks, and deep reds in the vegetable patch I use as their holding tank.

I meant to move them in March, but got too busy with work. Then, like a Biblical plague, the drought and heat settled in, so I told myself to wait for the fall. And, fortunately, the rains came. But somehow building a house—and a relationship—has kept my roses waiting.

So here I am, with three stone walls, waiting for spring. I pull out my catalogues and start looking for 'Roseraie de l'Haÿ.' This time, I will plant her to stay.

Henry Mitchell's 'Ginny'

ALLEN LACY

Henry Mitchell's 'Ginny'

I HAVE ABSOLUTELY NO DOUBT that America's best twentieth-century writer about gardens and the things that go on there was Henry Mitchell. For more than twenty years, right up to the time of Mitchell's death in 1993, subscribers to the *Washington Post* could turn to his "Earthman" columns to find out what was on his mind about the events in his Washington, D.C., garden. The garden was squeezed onto a lot just 40 by 187 feet, much of it occupied by his house. But it was crammed with plants, and there was never any lack of things to write about.

Mitchell's prose style and the personal voice that came through in it were so highly distinctive that no one who had read a few of his columns would need a byline to recognize his work. He was passionate, highly opinionated, sometimes quirky or cantankerous, and often very funny. He was to American garden literature pretty much what Mark Twain was to American writing in general: endlessly quotable. Marigolds? They should be "used as sparingly as ultimatums." The sunflower? It "is an American flower. It would do quite well, as far as I am concerned, as the national flower." The unalloyed pleasures of gardening? "It is not nice to garden anywhere. Everywhere there are violent winds, startling once-per-century floods, unprecedented droughts, record-setting freezes, abusive and blasting heats never known before. There is no place, no garden, where these terrible things do not drive gardeners mad."

People clipped his columns to save, and copied them to send to friends who were so unfortunate as to live where the *Washington Post* was not easily available. That was how I first became aware that there was a man named Henry Mitchell who was writing about gardening and with a rambunctiousness that made him a national treasure. And yet Mitchell himself consistently entertained a perverse and entirely unwarranted modesty about his writing. If told that a column was "a classic," he would retort that the writings of Shakespeare were classics, that his own scribblings were just newspaper pieces, of little if any interest a day or two after they came out.

It was *The Essential Earthman: Henry Mitchell on Gardening*, a collection of his pieces published by Indiana University Press in 1981, that brought its author national recognition. The book did not come into being in the usual way, however. Usually when someone publishes a collection of journalistic pieces it is because the author has decided that his or her columns have reached a certain critical mass and that they are worthy of preservation. The inspiration for *The Essential Earthman* was not Mitchell's. It belonged to John Gallman, an editor at Indiana who wanted to publish Mitchell's columns. Mitchell didn't gather together an assortment and mail them off. Gallman had to come to Washington to get them, and it was he, not Mitchell, who decided which to publish and how they should be arranged. Without Gallman, *The Essential Earthman* would never have seen the light of day.

But it did, and it proved to be a grand success. It didn't outsell Stephen King, but it was very well reviewed, and the subsequent history of editions showed it to be, in fact, a classic. It was brought out in paperback in 1983 by Farrar, Straus and Giroux. Houghton Mifflin published it in a new hardbound edition in 1992, and in paperback in 1999. And, just recently, Indiana University Press has reprinted it.

Mitchell, however, remained modest after the success of his book. A few years after its initial publication, his wife, Ginny, found four unanswered letters from editors wanting to publish another "Earthman" collection. When Ginny urged him to comply with one of these requests, his answer was that no one wanted to read these things, that they were worthless. "Well, I don't think so," she replied. "I'd like to buy the rights."

"Okay," he said. "They're yours. For one dollar." It was, then, through Ginny that Frances Tenenbaum, who had developed such an impressive list of gardening books that Houghton Mifflin gave her her own imprint, ended up with the rights to reprint *The Essential Earthman* as well as the collections *One Man's Garden* in 1994 and *Henry Mitchell on Gardening* in 1998.

Although roses have an enormous prominence in Henry Mitchell's writings, I would hesitate to describe him as a rose-lover.

First, he was not a floral sectarian (someone who elevates one genus of plants over all others), but a flower-lover of catholic tastes who reveled in many different plants—in sumptuous dahlias, in tree peonies, in daffodils and tulips and crocuses. (Writing in "Earthman," he had this to say: "Let us have no more talk about 'fat Dutch crocuses' or 'fat Dutch hyacinths'—as if the better sort of gardener loved only the slender, elegant wild crocuses and hyacinths unfed, unbred, and untouched by the Dutch. The truth is that nothing is more sprightly than to see patches of fat Dutch crocuses in March, coming as they do to lift our spirits and amaze the young and simple.")

Second, he minced no words in pointing out that all roses shared some faults. "Rose fanatics, needless to say, easily persuade themselves that this plant, the rose, has a wider range of color and form than any other plant, which is nonsense. They even go so far as to imagine that the bush itself is handsome, though the average rosebush is as nearly ugly as anything in the floral kingdom."

And, third, some kinds or types of roses just plain irritated him, particularly hybrid teas. He liked 'Sutter's Gold,' 'Helen Traubel,' and 'Mojave,' but these were exceptions to his general view that hybrid teas were more notable for flaws than virtues. Too often they were deficient in fragrance and susceptible to disease and winter cold. Too often they had been bred to bear gigantic flowers that were entirely out of scale. What possible good was there in a rose with huge flowers? Mitchell's dark suspicion was that the answer lay in rose shows and their competition for blue ribbons. "There is nothing wrong, or at least nothing utterly evil, in raising scentless roses that require weekly spraying and that can be sheltered and shielded, patted and pampered, until at last an enormous flower can be entered in a rose show. Without rose shows, and without roses that have never been outside an intensive care unit, society would suffer. Many people who are now safely occupied with the care of roses would be loose on the streets."

Anyone who follows the commercial rose industry and its annual introductions of new cultivars knows that the word "great" is used lavishly. In Mitchell's view, this adjective often could be translated to mean "some showy feature, usually blatant color or freak size, that endear[s] a rose to people who can see nothing unless it is inescapably obvious." And he got down to specifics with some hybrid teas that were great commercial successes, such as 'Chrysler Imperial' and 'Peace.' 'Chrysler Imperial' was a deep-red rose introduced in 1952, and the first plant to be named for an object of conspicuous consumption, in this case a tail-finned gas-guzzler. Mitchell's opinion of 'Chrysler Imperial' amounted to a pronounced harrumph: it is "precisely the sort of rose I dislike, with all those petals—when it blooms I always feel that I have witnessed an upheaval rather than a flowering." He disliked 'Peace' even more.

Now, in my own view, 'Peace' has some considerable merits. I do not grow it now. (I gave up hybrid teas years ago as too much trouble.) But at one time I found room for 'Peace.' Its foliage is uncommonly handsome—shiny, deep green, almost leathery—and it is somewhat resistant to disease. Its buds are long and pointed, and they open into huge, sumptuous blossoms of peachy pink suffused with apricot yellow. It has an interesting history, and it is possibly the best-selling rose of all time. But Mitchell never confused popularity or commercial success with true merit. Of 'Peace,' he wrote, "It has huge flowers that should please anyone who has always longed to grow the largest turnip in the world."

Henry Mitchell's ardent dislike of hybrid teas, some of them in particular, was matched by his love of other classes and some specific cultivars. He was enamored of the old roses, the historic *alba*s and musks and *gallica*s and *centifolia*s and damasks. He loved the roses derived from *Rosa rugosa* and *R. wichuraiana*, and all those nineteenth-century shrub roses named for respectable middle-class French-women. And his appreciation for climbers and ramblers bordered on ecstasy. "The most overpowering time of year in my garden is when the rambler and climbing roses bloom," he wrote in "Rosy Outlook," an essay in the posthumous collection *Henry Mitchell on Gardening*. He continues, "Not even azaleas, not even masses of tall bearded irises, produce such a sense of opulence, and this is no doubt because the masses of bloom are borne from ground level to fifteen feet in the air." In this piece, perhaps his final writing about roses, he traces his steps on a late afternoon in May as he walks from his back door to the alley. The path is lined with the roses he loves best, roses that make up for all the deficiencies he discerns in hybrid teas.

I am quite satisfied as I walk the hundred or so feet from the kitchen to the alley. First, to the left is a bush of the *rugosa* rose 'Belle Poitevine,' a fragrant blowsy pink bush with a good bit of blue in the rose color. Just ahead and nearer the walk is a twelve-foot-high bush of the *rugosa* 'Mrs. Anthony Waterer,' bred from the highly perfumed old hybrid perpetual 'Général Jacqueminot,' as fragrant as its parent. At its full height it leans into a fragrant white rambler, 'Seagull,' which clothes and arches over the walk. A few feet beyond is the nineteenth-century creamy white fragrant rambler 'Aglaia,' with the scentless purple rambler 'Violette' growing into it from the other side. The white is almost finished before the purple blooms. Their flowering overlaps only a few days. 'Aglaia' has clusters of double flowers that open all together in such a mass that the leaves are hidden, as is true of most old ramblers. But 'Seagull' opens its semidouble clusters of inch-wide dead white flowers little by little, giving a starry-night effect for several days until the whole plant is solid white. Beyond, on either side of the walk, are fat bushes about seven feet high of the white hybrid musk 'Moonlight,' which blooms off and on till frost. To the sides, thirty feet off, is the large-flowered climber 'Madame Grégoire Staechelin,' with ruffled, perfumed flowers showing a deeper rose on the reverse of the petals.

In his walk amidst the perfumes of a May afternoon, Mitchell continues his catalogue of roses. Before he reaches the last rose, 'Mme Plantier,' he greets

'Blossomtime,' 'Variegata di Bologna,' 'The Garland,' and others. But two roses require special attention. One is "a white multiflora rambler, quite fragrant, that might be mistaken for the wild *Rosa multiflora*, but that actually came from the garden of the late Mrs. Frederick Keys in Maryland, who did much to start the interest in old roses decades ago." The other, which is a little puzzling, is 'Ginny,' described as a "perfumed pink rambler."

'Ginny' is puzzling because there is a rose registered with the official name 'Ginny,' but it is not a rambler. It is a miniature. Its flowers are not pink, but red and white. This rose, bred by Francis J. Pischoff and introduced in 1981, has forty-five petals and is a cross between two other miniatures with cutesy names, 'Little Darling' and 'Toy Charm.' Now, one rose may have several names, as 'Peace' does. ('Mme Grégoire Staechelin' is sometimes sold as 'Spanish Beauty.') But two roses cannot share the same name, not according to the authorities who preside over nomenclatural questions. If the American Rose Society had gotten wind of Henry Mitchell's desire to name a rose 'Ginny,' when there already was a rose of that name, they would have disapproved—maybe sent him a letter ordering him to cease and desist. I also suspect that he would have snapped his fingers and said that the Society had no business interfering with the name he gave a rose he had raised from a seed. I understand such defiance. Years ago I stumbled upon an exceptionally lovely deep-violet-purple New England aster. It came to me without a name. Now it's widely sold in America as 'Hella Lacy.'

The story of Henry Mitchell's 'Ginny' can be pieced together from tidbits found here and there in his essays. He arranged a cross between two of his favorite roses. One was 'Mme Grégoire Staechelin,' that perfumed pink climber already mentioned. This rose was bred in Spain by Pedro Dot and introduced in 1921. It blooms only once, for about three weeks in late spring. The other was 'Dortmund,' hybridized in Germany by Wilhelm Kordes and introduced in 1955. It is remarkable for both foliage and flower. The leaves are dark green and almost as glossy as holly. The flowers are single and bright red with contrasting white centers. It will rebloom if deadheaded after the first flowering. Mitchell planted seeds, and there was one that he liked so much he decided to name it for his wife. However, he had some questions about the true parentage of his 'Ginny.' It was pink and fragrant, like 'Mme Grégoire,' and it was single like 'Dortmund,' but there was room for doubt about the exact ancestry.

Now, I happen to have been growing Mitchell's 'Ginny' since 1993, and I have a hypothesis to offer. The seed it grew from was contained in a hip on 'Mme Grégoire.' Some 'Dortmund' pollen may have been dusted on the good 'Mme's' pistil, but a bumblebee got there first. It brought a hearty masculine hello from another rose in the Mitchell garden, that *multiflora* rambler from the Maryland garden of the late Mrs. Frederick Keys. I cannot prove my hypothesis, but I will stick to it. I used to have a horrid hedge of wild *multiflora*s. Henry's 'Ginny' has a family resemblance. It flowers in clusters, and it bears small hips of blackish red. But its flowers are larger than those of the species, and they are much more fragrant, as well as a lovely soft pink instead of dirty white.

Here's how 'Ginny' came to be in my garden.

A couple of months after Henry Mitchell died of cancer, the National Arboretum in Washington put on a memorial tribute honoring his work. Hella and I attended. Our friend Frances Tenenbaum, who had been a close friend of Henry and Ginny as well as Henry's editor, came down from Boston. Frances introduced us to Ginny. We could see immediately why she had a rose named in her honor. As we were talking, a truly elegant woman in a blue denim dress joined us. It was Katharine Graham, the publisher of the *Washington Post* and a person I deeply admire for many good reasons. After half an hour, Kay Graham left, and Ginny Mitchell said she needed to get something for me from her car. It was that rose. "Henry named this for me," she said, "and he'd be happy to know that it will grow in somebody else's garden."

And it does. It's our only rose, and we're always glad when late May rolls around and we can enjoy its clouds of small, five-petaled, fragrant pink flowers.

Rosa 'Mme Hardy'

MICHAEL POLLAN

'Mme Hardy' and 'Cuisse de Nymphe'

P TO NOW, I've always avoided growing roses—*real* roses, that is; I've always had a tough climber or two. After all, who courts such captious and intimidating guests? But this spring for some reason the ripe catalogue shots of roses I always used to sail right past took hold in my imagination, and I decided to take the plunge. I think it must have been the two-page spread of "old-fashioned" roses in the Wayside catalogue that first seduced me. Here were a dozen ladies (and one debonair gent: 'Jacques Cartier') that looked nothing like roses were supposed to look. Instead of the trite, chaste, florist-shop bud, these large, shrubby plants bore luxuriant blooms that seemed to cascade down from the page: unruly masses of flower petals—hundreds of petals in some of them—just barely contained by form, which in most cases was that of a rosette or a teacup's half-globe. The whole effect was vaguely lascivious.

Dazzled, smitten, I ordered four old roses from Wayside. 'Mme Hardy,' of course; 'Jacques Cartier,' an 1868 introduction who looks quite suave in all his pictures; 'Königin von Dänemark' ("a jewel beyond price," and so presumably a bargain at $17.75); and 'Blanc Double de Coubert,' an 1892 hybrid *rugosa* that

Gertrude Jekyll considered "the whitest rose known." From another firm, I ordered a rose Wayside did not then carry, 'Maiden's Blush,' a shell-pink *alba* about which the catalogue copy was unequivocal: "Nature has created nothing more exquisite in plant or bloom."

The afternoon my old roses arrived by UPS truck, they seemed little more than sticks to me. They were completely dormant, and, apart from a faint swelling at the buds, they looked dead. Hard to believe I had dropped a total of seventy-five bucks on these twigs. The plants looked like two octopi joined at the head, the roots coming out one side and the canes the other. The idea, according to the directions, was to set the head (really the bud union) on top of a cushion of soil and spread the roots down along the sides. Here, in my Zone 5 Connecticut garden, Wayside recommends burying the bud union of a new rosebush at least two inches beneath the surface to protect it from winter stress. I checked the depth of the holes I had dug, carefully placed each rose, and then filled with soil, administering a final deep soak to ensure complete contact between the roots and the surrounding earth. After a few days of moisture, the roses would break their dormancy. The roots would send their delicate tentacles deep into the underlying mound of earth, and the alchemy by which the rose promised to translate this black mass of manure and decayed vegetable matter into blooms of legendary beauty would begin.

After only a few days, the buds reddened and swelled, and by the end of two weeks, the canes had unfurled around themselves a deep-green cloak of leaves—paler, daintier, and in finish more matte than the high-gloss foliage of modern roses. I had read that most old roses flower on "old wood" (last season's growth), so I had no expectation of blooms that first season. But in late June, after a month of rapid growth, 'Mme Hardy' sent forth a generous spray of buds. By then I had read so much about old roses that I frankly doubted they could live up to their billing. But 'Mme Hardy' was beautiful. From a small, undistinguished bud emerged a tightly wound bundle of pure, porcelain-white petals that were held in a perfect half-globe as if by an invisible teacup. The petals were innumerable yet not merely a mass: more ladylike than that, the fine tissue of 'Mme Hardy's' petals was subtly composed into the quartered form of a rosette, and the blooms made me think of the rose windows of Gothic cathedrals, which had not before looked to me anything like a rose.

It was hard to look at 'Mme Hardy' plain, hard not to think of her as an expression of another time—which of course, as much as being an expression of nature, she is. Though 'Mme Hardy' did not appear until 1832 (bred by the Empress Josephine's head gardener at Malmaison, and named for his wife), she embodies the classic form of old roses, and comes closer to the image the word "rose" has conjured in people's minds for most of Western history than do the roses in our florist shops today. To look closely at the bloom of an antique rose is, at least in some small way, an exercise of the historical imagination. You see it through your own eyes, yet also through the eyes of another time. What an odd thing, though, for a rose is not a poem, or a painting, but a flower, part of nature, timeless. Yet man in some sense made 'Mme Hardy,' crossed and recrossed it until it reflected his ideal of beauty—and so today in my garden it reflects the sensibility of another time back at me, a part of nature, but also a part of us.

Admiring the beauty of 'Mme Hardy' I began to see why she should so excite rosarians of a snobbish bent—and to accept the slightly uncomfortable fact that, at least in the war of the roses, my own sympathies were not with the party of the people. For, compared with modern roses, 'Mme Hardy' is indeed an aristocrat, incomparably more subtle and, in form, so much more *poised*, than, say, 'Dolly Parton,' with her huge blossoms.

Once you have grown old roses, you can begin to understand why people might project metaphors of social class onto them. Each bush itself forms a kind of social hierarchy. Beneath 'Mme Hardy's' bud union is the rootstock of another, tougher variety—not a hybrid but a rude species rose, some hardy peasant stock that can withstand bad winters, but whose meager flowers interest no one. The prized hybrid is grafted onto the back of this anonymous rootstock, which performs all the hard labor for the rose, working the soil, getting its roots dirty so that the plant may bloom. Although the prickly bush that results is not itself distinguished either, it, too, is necessary to support the luxury of the bloom. But the extravagant, splendid blooms, like true aristocrats, never seem to acknowledge the plant that supports them. They comport themselves as though their beauty and station were God-given, transcendent. You cannot discern in the bloom of a rose the work of the plant, the sacrifice of its chafer-eaten leaves, the stink of the manure in which it is rooted. "Roots?" 'Mme Hardy' asks ingenuously. "What roots?"

But if 'Mme Hardy' calls attention to her pedigree, 'Maiden's Blush,' the *alba* I planted beside her in my garden, seems to press her sexuality on us. Her petals are more loosely arrayed than 'Mme Hardy's,' less done up—almost unbuttoned. Her petals are larger, too, and they flush with the palest flesh-pink toward the center, which itself is elusive, concealed in the multiplication of her labial folds. The blush of this maiden is clearly not all in her face . . . Could I be imagining things? Well, consider some of the other names by which this rose is known: 'La Virginale,' 'Incarnata,' 'La Séduisante,' and . . . 'Cuisse de Nymphe.' This last is what the rose is called in France, where, as Vita Sackville-West tells us, blooms that blush a particularly deep pink are given the "highly expressive name" of 'Cuisse de Nymphe Emue,' which she demurs from translating. But there it is: the thigh of an aroused nymph.

To look at a flower and think of sex—what exactly can this mean? Emerson wrote that "Nature always wears the colors of the spirit," by which he meant that we don't see nature plain, only through a screen of human tropes. So, in our eyes, spring becomes youth, trees become truths, and even the humble ant becomes a big-hearted soldier. And certainly, when we look at roses and see aristocratic ladies or even Girl Scouts, or—on a higher level—symbols of love and purity, we are projecting human categories onto those roses, saddling them with the infinite burden of our metaphors.

In my garden this summer, 'Maiden's Blush' has flowered hugely, and some of her blossoms are flushed so deeply pink as to deserve the French appellation, 'Cuisse de Nymphe Emue.' Am I thinking metaphorically? Well, yes and no. This flower, like all flowers, *is*, after all, a sexual organ. The unlettered bumblebee seems to find this bloom just as attractive as I do: he seems just as bowled over by its perfume. Yet I can't believe I gaze at the blossom in quite the same way he does. Its allure, for me, has to do with its resemblance to women—put frankly, to "the thighs of an aroused nymph," about which I must assume the bumblebee feels nothing. For this is a resemblance my species has bred this rose to have. So are my ideas imaginary? Merely a representation of my own psychology and desire? But what about the bee? That's no representation he is busy pollinating. Are we finally speaking of nature or culture when we speak of a rose (nature) that has been bred by men (culture) so that its blossoms (nature) make men imagine (culture) the sex of women (nature)?

It may be this sort of confusion that we need more of. Among plants, none supply it quite as well as the rose.

Rosa 'Mister Lincoln'

LAUREN SPRINGER

'Mister Lincoln' and 'Harison's Yellow'

⌒

T HIS IS A BRIEF STORY OF TWO ROSES, two roses that couldn't be more different. They share little besides basic rose genetics, an American pedigree, and my deepest affection.

'Harison's Yellow' is a scrappy old shrub, a thorny, twiggy, six-foot mound that for a brief week (or two, if the late-spring weather remains benevolently mild and still) festoons itself with brilliant sulfur-yellow semi-double flowers possessed of a crisp, not-too-sweet fragrance. This American hybrid between the Scots burnet, *Rosa pimpinellifolia*, and the Austrian briar, *Rosa foetida*, is lovable in its simplicity, resourceful adaptability, and unpretentiousness—a perfect rose to reflect the spirit of its day.

George Harison brought it into the trade in New York in the first half of the nineteenth century—in 1846, to be exact. Because of its tough, suckering nature, it was easily transported and transplanted across the country by settlers and forty-niners. Known as the Yellow Rose of Texas, it can still be found growing today in West Texas, but also all the way on up into the Dakotas, and from the Eastern Seaboard across to California. Tolerant of neglect, drought, harsh winds, intense heat, bitter cold, and poor soil, it grows just about anywhere. It graces charming old farmsteads and run-down trailer parks, cutting across cultural lines as well as geographical ones. It is truly an American plant. My respect for its hardy constitution and pleasure in its dependably bright display of bloom mirror my feelings for this country and her people.

I got my first bush from a potted-up piece at the home-donations booth of the annual Denver Botanic Gardens plant sale fourteen years ago, so the rose's pass-along tradition has carried on into my own garden. As I begin to make my third garden in Colorado, several tawny, vigorous, densely spined suckers will be dug out and transplanted. In just a few years, the plant will have grown into a sizable shrub with dense, small foliage and a fine-textured but unkempt habit.

In spite of my now having a smaller space to garden, I pay no heed to common sense, which tells me I shouldn't waste precious footage on a spreading rose that looks good for only a shy two weeks a year. There is a resonance to having a piece of American history in the garden, a plant that transcends mere horticulture and speaks of going west. I wonder who brought along the parent plant of the roses that I have grown, and what their life was like. I wonder where they planted their rose, and if it is still there. I wonder if they settled in that spot, or moved on. I, too, went west from the Eastern Seaboard to find happiness and opportunity, and to make a new life. I moved to a part of the United States that is rougher, wilder, harder to tame, harder to garden than where I grew up. 'Harison's Yellow' likes it here, and so do I. For, like this rose, I too am an American product of two European parents, one an Austrian. I'd like to think that both the rose and I have found an ideal part of the world in which to live and prosper, and yet I find no discomfort in knowing that both of us may move on again and continue to do well.

As for the short blooming period of 'Harison's Yellow,' there is something to be said in defense of plants that offer their best performance for only a little while. Some of us mark our lives by those transitory events in the garden, when fleeting flowers bloom, when fall foliage burns brilliant, when wild creatures make their annual appearance and later take their equally regular seasonal leave. The golden generosity of 'Harison's Yellow' comes dependably and all too briefly at the end of May in Colorado, like the broad smile on the face of an old friend you see but once a year. Would that smile shine as brightly if you saw it every day? Perhaps, but you might not notice after a while.

'Mister Lincoln' is an entirely different being from 'Harison's Yellow' in almost every way. Blooming continuously from late spring past several hard frosts in late autumn, it offers the most luxuriant, velvety red flowers in the elegant, high-centered, mysteriously furled style of its class, the hybrid teas. Opulently fragrant, with the olfactory richness and complexity one would expect from a dark-red tea rose, a single flower's thirty-five petals open into a graceful cup. Large but not vulgar, the flowers are held high on long-necked, strong stems above an upright, stiff, well-clothed three-foot shrub. The dark-green foliage has little or no sheen, a good quiet companion to the sensual flowers. The plant exudes class on all accounts. Thoroughly modern, this American-bred hybrid tea rose debuted in 1964 and became an instant classic and an All-America Rose Selections winner. But it does share attributes with its distant cousin 'Harison's Yellow.' Vigorous, healthy, tolerant of some shade and lousy soil conditions, it is one of the most persistently popular hybrid teas to this day, as much because of its easygoing nature as its beauty.

Now, I must say that I am not generally a fan of modern roses, especially the hybrid teas and floribundas. Their gawky habit, generally strong need for ongoing maintenance, and often scentless flowers all turn me off. I spent several years growing and processing them for the cut-flower trade under glass, and tending to formal gardens filled with hundreds of them on an estate. It was soulless work somehow, marked by chemicals and other unnatural interventions. It had little to do with seasonal cycles and much to do with control, spoiling two aspects of what I love most about gardening: participating in the bigger pattern of life and relinquishing my actions to that pattern, or at least attempting to guide my actions in a synchronous rhythm. My affections lie firmly with the shrub and species roses, and the fragrant old garden roses such as the *gallica*s, *alba*s, and damasks.

But the first rose in my life was an ill-tended 'Mister Lincoln' my mother had bought bare-root at the local hardware store in Philadelphia, and stuck in partial shade by the hemlock beside our back porch. Stretching for light, fighting the encroaching lawn and crabgrass at its feet, and never receiving even a bucketful of water in the sweltering heat of a rainless August, or any form of food or winter protection, this rose persisted and bloomed faithfully, year after year. On holidays, my mother sent me out into the garden to collect whatever might serve as a floral arrangement. The late-autumn and winter holidays posed quite a challenge, and stretched both my observational abilities and my appreciation for evergreen foliage, twig form and pattern, dried flowers, and various nuts, seedheads, and berries. Many a Thanksgiving, however, I would be lucky enough to find a perfect dark-red bud of 'Mister Lincoln,' still held high on that old, lanky bush that had little to recommend it as a garden plant after our abuse and neglect. I was moved by the contrast of this homely plant and the beautiful flower it still managed to muster, that late in the season, once more, yet.

Just as there is something to be said for plants such as 'Harison's Yellow' that have only a brief moment of rapture each season, there is something special about an unremarkable-looking plant that produces something incongruously lovely. The plain, dusty, green arms of a night-blooming cereus droop over a chain-link fence in a Los Angeles barrio, sending out a huge creamy flower; the dull, almost lifeless leaves and scaly brown base of an orchid in my friend's greenhouse finally push forth a long stem of flowers otherworldly in their beauty and complexity; the warty gray sticks of an ocotillo in the New Mexican desert suddenly burst into brilliant red flowers. Our 'Mister Lincoln' was just like these, the plant world's version of a scurfy old oyster making its pearls. We may fill our gardens with the most comely plants, ones that bloom for months on end, with perfect form and unscathed foliage, with four seasons of interest and the like. But to refuse the charms of plants that don't fit this ideal, and to demand perfection from everything we plant—in doing this, we lose our ability to love what is most special in life: beauty that transcends expectation, judgment, or time, that comes into our lives when it will and transforms the moment. 'Harison's Yellow' and 'Mister Lincoln' have done that for me.

Rosa 'Eglantyne'

DAVID AUSTIN

'Eglantyne'

T HE SO-CALLED OLD ROSES reached the peak of their popularity in
the eighteenth and nineteenth centuries, and many beautiful varieties
have been preserved for our pleasure in the present day. Most of these
roses flower only once, in the early summer, though at the end of their period
of greatest popularity we began to get roses that flower throughout the summer.
These were the China roses, the Portland roses, the Bourbon roses, and the hybrid perpetuals. They had but a short taste of fame, however, for it was not long
before the hybrid teas took over, almost completely wiping the old roses off the
garden scene.

To my mind, this was a tragedy, for the old rose flower had, I would say, much
greater charm and beauty than the hybrid teas that we find in most gardens today. This development was particularly unfortunate because the repeat-flowering
old roses were never really developed to their full potential. Though they have an
undeniable beauty, they are often subject to disease, and they are by no means reliably repeat-flowering. Their color range is also limited, for there are virtually
no yellow, apricot, or peach shades. Crimson tends to be lacking as well in all

but the hybrid perpetuals, which themselves quickly moved toward the hybrid tea in flower and growth. All in all, there are no more than a few really good repeat-flowering old roses.

It was with these thoughts in mind that I set out to breed a new race of roses, which I have called the English roses. They are the result of crossing the old roses with modern hybrid teas and floribundas. They combine the unique character and beauty of the old roses with the excellent repeat-flowering qualities of modern roses. They also possess all the various colors that we find in modern roses, though the flower form is very much that of an old rose. The bloom may be cup-shaped or in the form of a rosette, often with numerous small petals, the light between the petals giving them a warm, glowing effect. Or the petals may turn downward, to provide a more domed flower. But whatever their shape, English roses have a particularly strong fragrance inherited from the old roses, for I have always been careful to breed almost exclusively from fragrant varieties. Among them, one may find not only the beautiful old rose aroma, but also the scent of some hybrid teas, the musk rose, myrrh, and many different fruits. I think it is no exaggeration to say that they are the most fragrant of all roses, not excluding the old roses themselves. English roses are in fact *new* old roses, if I may be forgiven for that apparent contradiction in terms.

English roses have a natural, shrubby growth, which makes them ideal plants for both the mixed border and the garden generally. Individual varieties may grow to four or five feet in height, or they may be quite short, no taller than a typical hybrid tea rose. They may have bushy growth or may be gracefully arching. A few are quite upright, making them suitable for placing behind other plants. Shorter varieties can be used for bedding, and some of the taller ones make excellent repeat-flowering climbers.

English roses are remarkably adaptable plants. They look particularly at home in a mixed border, for their sumptuous blooms provide a welcome contrast to the lighter and airier flowers of most herbaceous plants. It is not difficult to find hues among English roses that will exist in harmony with any color scheme. But it must be remembered that no rose likes too much competition, and it is advisable to surround them with plants that are not too robust. An entire border of

English roses is hard to beat for sheer exuberance of flower and fragrance. Some people prefer to use a limited range of harmonizing colors, perhaps using only the so-called cool shades of white, pink, crimson, and purple or, alternatively, the warm colors of yellow, bright red, apricot, and peach—though this is in no way a rule. In small borders, single plants are very satisfactory, but wherever possible we would always advise planting in groups of three or more of one variety, so that one plant grows into another to provide a bushier effect, and also to assure a more continuous flowering. When one plant has temporarily ceased to flower, another may take over.

For those who have sufficient space, it is possible to plant a rose garden entirely of English roses. Such a garden may follow the conventional form, or we might consider something more imaginative, perhaps two long borders facing a path and intersecting occasionally with other paths. In the U.K., such a garden would be in flower from June to October (longer in warmer climates) and provide a whole range of delicious fragrances.

One of the most important developments in English roses in recent years has been their use as climbers. Some of these may be described as true climbers, such as 'Malvern Hills,' 'A Shropshire Lad,' 'Mortimer Sackler,' 'Spirit of Freedom,' and 'William Morris.' Others are usually grown as shrubs but do in fact also make excellent climbers—for example, 'Graham Thomas,' 'The Pilgrim,' and 'Teasing Georgia.' English roses usually reach a height of about eight feet, which is ideal for people who do not wish to climb a ladder to prune them. English climbing roses are at their best on a wall, where they give a very long season of bloom, but they are also excellent on an arch or pillar.

English roses grown as standards can also be valuable in the garden, particularly in more formal areas. They are excellent for providing height, or they may be used as focal points, or perhaps for planting at regular intervals along the edge of a path. They also create a pleasing effect when allowed to grow above shorter herbaceous plants or roses in formal beds. When grown as standards, their beautiful flowers and rich and varied fragrances can be enjoyed at close quarters. But, being naturally wide and bushy, they form extra-large heads, so firm support in the form of a stout stake immediately after planting is essential.

English roses are ideal as cut flowers, too. They are less stiff in growth than most modern roses, and one can create a graceful arrangement with their attractively nodding flowers. With their numerous petals, they also tend to last a long time in water. There is almost no better way of enjoying the beauty and fragrance of the individual flowers than arranging them in a bowl for the house.

English roses have been in a continuous process of development now for more than thirty years, and it is inevitable that more recent varieties are greatly superior to some of the earlier ones, which are often no less beautiful but perform less well in gardens. Within the last decades, a favorite of mine has been 'Eglantyne,' one of the most beautiful of all our English roses. The flawless form of its flowers and their soft overall appearance seem to me to represent the very essence of an old rose. The blooms are a delicate pink, richer toward the center, and are perfectly borne, the petals turning up a little at the edges in an almost saucerlike shape. They are sweetly scented with a charming and delicate old rose fragrance. 'Eglantyne' is related to 'Mary Rose,' which in turn has connections with the *rugosa* roses. This kinship has given it a form that is ideal, with rich, healthy foliage, a nice, twiggy, bushy growth to medium height, and little disease, making it an excellent garden plant. It was named for a wonderful lady, Eglantyne Jebb, who was born in the county where our nursery is situated, and was the founder of the Save the Children Fund during the First World War.

Taken all in all, 'Eglantyne' typifies the unique charm of the English roses, representing the vigor, disease resistance, fragrance, and beauty we are trying to create. Of the more than nine hundred varieties our nursery currently offers, it is one of the best.

Rosa 'Golden Wings'

THOMAS FISCHER

A Trio of Single Roses: 'Mrs Oakley Fisher,'
'Golden Wings,' and 'Darlow's Enigma'

W ITH A GROUP OF PLANTS as large and multifarious as roses, it's only natural that a gardener should want to sample as many varieties as possible. That is a polite way of saying that my morals are somewhat loose. I'll admit, when it comes to roses, there have been times when the traffic in and out of my garden must have looked suspiciously heavy. But there are mitigating circumstances—my garden is less than a quarter-acre in size, and the sunny area suitable for growing roses a mere fragment of that fragment. I have no choice but to practice serial rose polygamy. If that saddles me with a reputation for being a little, well, slutty, so be it.

Things could be worse, I suppose. Like Madame Alvarez, the elderly former courtesan in Colette's *Gigi*, I can look back on my youthful *liaisons du coeur* with a sigh of bittersweet pleasure. First there was the fling with old roses, their pinks and crimsons so sumptuous and velvety, their perfumes so intense—but, alas, their period of bloom so brief. Then came an extended dalliance with the hybrid musks—such masses of flowers, such subtle, pearly colors. Ah, yes, I remember them well—what a pity they had to go to make room for other plants.

Having accumulated an impressive number of notches on my garden gate-post, I've arrived at a point when it takes more than a pretty face to turn my head. Because my garden is so small, any rose I plant has to bloom all season—no three- or four-week wonders, no matter how brilliant their flowers. And since my sunny border is decidedly mixed, I insist on well-clothed, substantial shrubs that look good with a wide range of perennials, annuals, bulbs, and climbers—a cluster of gaunt sticks is not my idea of a proper rose. A couple of other personal quirks have further narrowed the list of candidates. I grow lots of blue flowers, and I don't like the way they look next to pink or red, so I want only roses that are white, yellow, orange, or apricot. Finally, I strive for a "German" rather than an English look in my border, which means that there are lots of ornamental grasses and airy, small-flowered perennials. Next to such svelte bordermates, big fat double roses would look gross and out of place. So the roses need to be single-flowered, or, at most, small and semi-double. Good resistance to black spot and powdery mildew are also requirements that are nonnegotiable.

So—what does this rather fussy and unreasonable list of demands leave us with? As it turns out, a trio of charming roses that have done all I've asked of them and then some. Let's start with the oldest and work our way forward.

Bred by the English rosarian Benjamin Cant and released in 1921, 'Mrs Oakley Fisher' is usually classified as a hybrid tea. Officially, I despise most hybrid teas, which fall into the "cluster of gaunt sticks" category as far as I'm concerned, and compound the offense by bearing large double flowers. But 'Mrs Oakley Fisher' defies the stereotype. First of all, she will assume shrublike proportions, given the chance. But it's the flowers that most effectively neutralize the hybrid-tea curse. Opening from pointed, deep-orange buds, the blossoms are five-petaled, about three inches across, and of a subtle, almost fleshlike apricot, with beautifully contrasting orange stamens. (Yet another reason to grow single roses: you get to see the stamens.) There's a lovely fragrance, too. I could be having olfactory hallucinations, but the perfume seems stronger to me when the flowers are in bud than when they're open. To top it off, the foliage is a glossy, deep bronze, which chimes quite nicely with the flowers. In my border, early summer sees 'Mrs Oakley Fisher' backed by medium-blue delphiniums, with

Penstemon heterophyllus 'True Blue' around her knees; later on, *Salvia patens* takes over from the penstemons, and the delphiniums have a resurgence in late August or early September. All the while, 'Mrs Oakley Fisher' has been blooming away, looking as fresh and elegant as I'm sure her namesake must have done, eighty-some years ago.

It's always interesting, I think, to know a rose's parentage. This has nothing to do with social snootiness, as it does in human contexts ("Who *are* your mother's people?"), but, rather, with knowing what to expect from the plant in terms of habit, foliage, flower appearance, frequency of bloom, fragrance (or the lack of it), and resistance to disease. For example, if a rose has a lot of *Rosa rugosa* in its ancestry, you can bet that it will be hardy, spicily fragrant, and rugged as hell. A large proportion of *R. foetida* genes, on the other hand, may confer brilliant yellow or orange coloration, but will also probably mean a high susceptibility to black spot.

Sadly, the parentage of 'Mrs Oakley Fisher' is unknown, but of the second member of my trio, 'Golden Wings,' there is much to tell. Bred by the American rose historian Roy Shepherd and released in 1956, 'Golden Wings' resulted from a cross between the hybrid tea 'Soeur Thérèse' and a seedling of the Scots-briar (*R. pimpinellifolia* 'Grandiflora') crossed with the primary hybrid 'Ormiston Roy' (*R. pimpinellifolia* × *R. xanthina*). The first thing to notice here is that there's a lot of yellow going on. 'Soeur Thérèse' has double, deep-yellow flowers edged in carmine, *R. pimpinellifolia* 'Grandiflora' has single, primrose-yellow flowers, and 'Ormiston Roy' has single, buttercup-yellow flowers. So, as you might expect, their child, 'Golden Wings,' has creamy yellow flowers. (A double dose of *R. pimpinellifolia* DNA can also be seen lurking behind the mid-green foliage, profuse prickliness, and pleasant, light fragrance of 'Golden Wings.')

The odds would also seem to have favored single flowers over the double flowers of 'Soeur Thérèse,' and so they did. But the genetic scrambling that occurs in every instance of sexual reproduction can produce surprises. Even though 'Soeur Thérèse' couldn't prevail in the single-versus-double contest, she did win out in another important area: length of bloom. Like most species roses, *R. pimpinellifolia* blooms only once a year, in late spring or early summer;

THOMAS
FISCHER

'Ormiston Roy,' being the offspring of two once-blooming species, also blooms only once a year. As a hybrid tea, however, 'Soeur Thérèse' carries the genes for repeat blooming, and, as luck would have it, she passed them on to 'Golden Wings.' Maybe it *does* matter, after all, who your mother's people are.

In my garden, 'Golden Wings' grows about four feet tall and wide, filling a large space (and keeping the peace) between a twelve-foot specimen of *Cornus controversa* 'Variegata' and a clump of the boldly striped ornamental grass *Miscanthus sinensis* 'Cosmopolitan'; nearby, the rather floppy herbaceous *Clematis* × *jouiniana* 'Praecox' erupts in small pale-blue flowers for many weeks, and *Persicaria polymorpha*—one of the best and most tractable of the knotweeds—sports ivory plumes from early June until late August. It's the rose, however, that holds this group together. (One hint: continuous bloom with 'Golden Wings' is greatly aided by removing the spent flowers, although if you don't you'll get an autumn display of large reddish-orange hips as compensation for the reduced number of flowers.)

With the third and newest of my single roses, we move from an open book, genetically speaking, to an enigma—'Darlow's Enigma,' to be exact. All that seems to be known about this rose is that it was discovered by a man named Michael Darlow in his garden in Eugene, Oregon, sometime in the early 1990s. Furthermore, there's no agreement about what kind of rose it is. Some nurseries classify it as a hybrid musk; others (including Heirloom Roses, from whom I got my plant) as a rambler. One Web page even claims that it's an "improved" form of that vile weed *R. multiflora.* On the basis of my limited experience, I cast my vote with those who put it in the hybrid-musk category—it has the upright stance; small dark-green leaves; dense clusters of small semi-double flowers; and a sweet, far-traveling scent that I associate with that admittedly rather vaguely defined group. If that were all 'Darlow's Enigma' offered, it would be nice enough, but not in any way superior to classic hybrid musks like 'Cornelia' or 'Penelope.'

There are several howevers, however. For one thing, it's always covered in creamy-white flowers from June into the fall, *without deadheading*. You'll never need to touch it with your Felcos unless an errant cane—and it *is* vigorous, growing to ten feet or more—gets in the way. For another thing, it's one of the hardiest of shrub roses, suffering only minor dieback in USDA Zone 4. For a third, it never shows a speck of mildew or black spot. And, most remarkably, it will bloom well even in the shade, as long as you don't subject it to dank, Stygian gloom.

I have my plant of 'Darlow's Enigma' wedged between two purple smoke bushes that get cut back annually, and that seems a good place for it—the new growth of the smoke bushes keeps the rose in bounds (to a certain extent), and the purple foliage makes a handsome contrast with the white roses. Few pairings in my garden have lasted as long or provide as much pleasure. Given my proclivities, I may not always have 'Darlow's Enigma,' but whenever I'm reminded of it, I'll think of Madame Alvarez, fondly recalling those long-ago affairs.

Rosa 'Astrid Lindgren'

LLOYD BRACE

'Astrid Lindgren'

❧

Y APPRECIATION FOR 'ASTRID LINDGREN' is bound up with my
short career as a rose merchant. For ten years I sought and sold
plants under the motto "Practical Roses for Hard Places," meaning
roses that would be cane-hardy at least in my mid-coast Maine venue in Zone
5b. This enterprise, which ceased with my retirement at the end of 2002, was
aimed at a growing portion of the gardening public in northerly places who are
chary of using "ten syllable" chemicals, rose cones, and extensive late-winter
pruning. This ruled out hybrid teas and most floribundas, both of which are still
America's most popular types. But it left a broad palette of species, the old garden roses, from *gallica*s to some of the hybrid perpetuals, plus *rugosa*s, many climbers, and modern shrubs.

Since Genesis, when God granted to humankind hegemony over the world
and its flora and fauna, we of the West have taken His cue almost into our genes,
with results that leave this unchurched observer mostly underwhelmed. I have
heard this mandate, as it devolves upon roses, expressed hundreds of times in my
customers' desire for the impossible: "a Zone 3 yellow climber that blooms con-

stantly from Memorial Day to Columbus Day, has a suffocatingly strong old-garden-rose scent, produces gorgeous hips, is impervious to black spot, both mildews, and rust, is poisonous to aphids, sawflies, and thrips, never needs pruning, and only needs to be watered once a month." Predictably, I would also hear that if we can put a man on the moon . . .

The apotheosis of this command stance toward nature came with a prospect (fortunately, never a customer) who showed up at the nursery one day in high heels, a book of paint chips in hand. She explained that she had put in a swimming pool surrounded by a large patio of bluestone flags, upon which she had deployed a new set of outdoor furniture. Said furniture was of white tubing with woven plastic webbing of a plaid design that included a pink she would like to match in the blooms of roses roundabout. The color was right there in the middle of one of the color book's pages. I soon concluded that what she needed was two dozen of 'Jacques Cartier,' which the American Rose Society wants us to call 'Marchesa Boccella.' The lady liked the fact that it grew to five feet here in Maine and that it would bloom three times a season. I asked her just how tight her color specs were, since roses, like wine, are affected in their way by soil factors. She said that her standards were very high, and what did I mean? Told that the proposed rose—which was in bloom, matched the color, and had captivated her—could be anywhere on the color page in other soils, she huffed "Well!" and, at a loss for further words, stalked off the property. She was the exemplar of a distinction I make among customers: between exterior decorators and gardeners.

Of course, as a vendor trying to keep body and soul together, one can't go around dictating which varieties a customer shall have, though I must say I was always humbled but delighted when people asked me to use my taste and judgment to save them exhausting research. Most of the time, I would engage in a dialogue that would bring out the effect the prospect was trying for, his or her pet dislikes ("rugosas are trashy" or "once-bloomers are stupid"), and the conditions the plants would have to endure. I greatly enjoyed these encounters, and for the most part, I believe the customers did as well. Still, even with such reasonable people, there would often come a plaintive call for the super-rose. Frequently, 'Astrid Lindgren' would suffice.

This rose, introduced in 1991 and named by Poulsen of Denmark for the late children's-story author, is also known as 'Dream Sequence' in America, where it has not had much promotion and is, unfortunately, quite hard to find. That is what made it catch my eye at Hortico in Canada—that and its simple good looks. Though its parentage is unknown, 'Astrid Lindgren' combines aesthetics and vigor very successfully. The barely double blooms come mostly in clusters of three to five. They are cups about three and a half inches across and an inch and a half deep—in all, a form much like a gardenia. The velvety petals are a rich light pink that is infused with a bit of apricot near the center, which is graced with a boss of golden stamens. I would describe the fragrance as a combination of musk, fruit, and spice; at least one authority detects raspberry. Most roses that rebloom in my garden do so quite distinctly for about eighteen days in late June, around the beginning of August, and again after Labor Day. 'Astrid' starts for me in the third week of June and goes constantly and profusely for two months, past the middle of August. Then it starts up again in the second week of September and goes as late as the third week in October. As I write, in late November, most of the hundreds of potted rose varieties in my field have lost their leaves. Those of 'Astrid Lindgren' are not only intact but an active green, and there are still promising buds. The habit of 'Astrid Lindgren' as a shrub is tall and wide (six feet high by five feet wide), but if supported it will climb to at least eight feet. The thick medium-green foliage does not seem to know the meaning of mildew. On a scale of black-spot susceptibility from one for *rugosa* to ten for hybrid teas, I would put 'Astrid Lindgren' at four. She has earned a place in the garden of my dotage.

Of course I am not yet so decrepit that only one rose will suffice. I already have some 'George Vancouver,' 'Jens Munk,' *Rosa Rugosa* 'Magnifica,' 'Henry Hudson,' 'Blanc Double de Coubert,' 'Thérèse Bugnet,' and 'Fru Dagmar Hastrup' growing along the barn foundation and against the terrace built of big stones from part of it. After some landscaping to divert a major water flow in front of the house, I expect to plant a hedge of *rugosa*s, along with Scotsbriar, and species roses like *Rosa palustris*, and like *R. eglanteria*, along with 'Harison's Yellow,' and whatever else I find surviving in pots after this early and hard winter. I don't expect to have a rose garden per se, but simple, low-key accents that do not shout "design." I also want to venture into the worlds of lilacs, hardy azaleas, and rhododendrons, and various bird-attracting viburnums. Roses have kept me from beekeeping and vegetable gardening for ten years, so I will be back into those enterprises with gusto. And yet, as I leave the trade, a great infusion of new, hardy varieties is coming onto the market. With plenty of ground and time before me, I'm sure that more of those varieties will find their places. But 'Astrid Lindgren' will always be among them.

Rosa 'The Fairy'

CHRISTOPHER LLOYD

Roses at Great Dixter

⤸

THERE SEEMS TO BE A RUMOR ABROAD that I am against roses. To an extent, this is true, and I have, after all, had plenty of experience with them. An infinite vista of pain and frustration is conjured by my inward eye whenever I think of this ridiculously idolized shrub. Sentiment, rather than reality, is the basis of its popularity, and it seems to be wrapped up with the ego of its admirers. "Hate the rose and you are insulting me," is the message (of course, it could be intended).

I inherited a rose garden, and for years I was its slave. I pruned and trained roses. Every year, I sallied forth to some nearby wood that had been coppiced exactly two years before, and cut ash pegs wherewith to bend and secure, in a horizontal position, the long canes produced by two beds of Bourbon and hybrid perpetual roses—'Mme Isaac Pereire' was a favorite—so that they could make garlands of cabbagy blossom in due course. I mulched them assiduously, which did have the effect of combating black spot. If they were prone to mildew, I didn't grow them. They had to cope with aphids and wait for natural predators to do their work.

All the thanks I got was peals of maniacal laughter (you need supersensory vibes to be aware of that) every time they saw me appearing, secateurs at the ready. But it was they who were ready for me, lacerating me (gloves or no gloves) on every grabbable part of my anatomy. It was a particular joke with 'Easlea's Golden Rambler' to grab me in neck and back simultaneously.

Gaps would appear in my rose beds. Rather than replant the entire bed, I believed in plugging the gaps with varieties that I liked and had propagated myself, from cuttings (no suckers; very important, that). Sometimes these plants did well enough. At other times, they pined, though for what I knew not, until we heard about replant disease. Another imposition. I was instructed to replace the soil where each rose had previously grown. There is no spare soil in that part of the garden. What next?

What next was the arrival on the scene, ten years ago, of Fergus Garrett. I had spotted him when he was a horticultural student, young, muscular, and energetic, aged twenty-one or so. He had come with a party to see the garden. His hair was reddish. I was intrigued and asked him if it was dyed. It was, with henna (like the Masai tribe in Africa, you know). We became firm friends. Then, after a stint in France and Switzerland, he returned to England and agreed to become my head gardener. He is now thirty-eight and has transformed my life— starting with that rose garden. There was the joyful tearing sound of protesting, rending roots as he proceeded with the work of destruction, and, joy oh joy, I was free.

Roses hated it there, anyway. It is the hottest spot in my garden. They wilted in the heat. But, believe me (if you can), I'm not silly about roses. I like some of them, on my own terms, very much, but not all herded together, so that they all catch the same diseases through proximity, like children in a school. Also so that you are remorselessly aware of their ugly habit, whereas under mixed-border conditions, which is the way I most like to include them, their defects are concealed by their neighbors.

Actually, if the truth be told, I like roses best when they are at their brief best, in your garden rather than mine. I will gladly visit you then, swoon in the palpable aura of the scent, but leave before they fade and hold on to their dead petals, while later blooms in the truss vainly attempt to compete with the gathering decay about them.

Roses are steeped in nostalgia and sentiment, and even I, one of the least sentimental of gardeners, am a little bit subject to this weakness, which is such a deterrent to much-needed change (look at the British, with their silly pound sterling, making them refuse to join a more global monetary system). So I stick by my single-flowered pillar rose 'Irish Elegance,' with salmony blooms, especially pretty in the bud. For about two days in the year, it really is rather charming, and it was there before I was born.

So was the China, 'Comtesse du Caÿla.' My parents had two large beds of it—a semi-double salmony rose that smells delicately of China tea. I am a great one for doing a job when I'm in the mood, which isn't necessarily when it is most wisely done. At the tail end of 1946, I pruned those two beds quite hard. There followed the hardest winter in memory, and a large number were killed. About half a dozen of those that survived, remain. Fergus likes them. I sort of do.

'Léonie Lamesch' is a curious old floribunda-type rose that remains a sentimental relic. The bush of single apricot-colored 'Mrs Oakley Fisher' I struck from a cutting given me by Vita Sackville-West. I couldn't possibly let that go, could I? And I have one plant left of the hybrid musk 'Moonlight,' which has purple young foliage but trusses of white flowers. It is normally seen as a perfectly ordinary shrub, but mine found itself next to what became a tree of the variegated Portugal laurel, *Prunus lusitanica*. Rather then be swamped by it, this gallant little rose accepted the challenge and has climbed fifteen feet into the top of its partner, from which it peeps out as a wholly unexpected adornment. I love that, and it does it a second time, in autumn.

There are a few roses that I cling to largely because no one else is offering them anymore. Such are the pressures of more and still more novelties that some of the slightly older ones simply have to drop out of the lists, good or not. The bush floribunda (which I would call a *polyantha*) 'Madge' is one of these. Twice in a year, it carries abundant clusters of sweetly scented (of *Rosa arvensis*) white pompoms. It is a sweetie, but as no one else is interested, we propagate it ourselves, from cuttings, for our own small nursery. Another is 'Florence May

Morse,' which makes a pillar up to eight feet or so. The clustered flowers are carried almost continuously for five months, and it is a wonderful mixed-border ingredient. Red is a color that's in short supply among hardy perennials from July on (monardas are hopelessly prone to mildew nowadays, and *Lychnis chalcedonica* has too brief a season). This rose fills the need, and I have spaced three specimens along my Long Border. The clustered flowers are no great shakes as to shape (no pedigree there, I fear), but they are a straightforward red and contribute just what I need in a border that is entirely eclectic in its varied ingredients.

You may say that the floribunda 'The Fairy' is hackneyed and seen everywhere, but I'm no snob (or only slightly snobbish, anyway), and not only is 'The Fairy' a pleasing shade of clear pink, none too easily found ('Bonica' has it, too, and I have a bush of that), but its leaves have a healthy gloss. It flowers over a long period and blends excellently—for instance, with the white Chinese chives, *Allium tuberosum*, which seeds into and through it; and with other blenders, like *Viola cornuta* hybrids. I want my garden to be a tapestry, not a series of incidents.

I gather that Dan Hinkley has written here about *rugosa* roses, but I shall surely not be treading on his toes if I express my appreciation of the true *rugosa*s, like the single-flowered 'Alba,' with its splendid pale-green rugose foliage, simple (scented) flower, and tomato hips. Compare that with the miserable 'Blanc Double de Coubert,' only grown, I guess, so that connoisseurs can roll its classy name off their tongue (usually getting it wrong, but never mind). The leaves are nothing to compare with the true *rugosa*s, and there are no fruits. Furthermore, at least in my country, the flowers are nearly always blotched with dead brown patches, even when still in bud. I loathe this pretentious nitwit.

Shall I end in this trough, or shall I try to clamber out of the mire? Well, there are some fruiting roses that I should hate to be without. In its way, the sweet briar, *R. rubiginosa*, is unbeatable. Not just the apple scent, carried far on the air, but its trusses of brilliant scarlet hips. Do you prune it correctly? Do you prune any of your shrub roses correctly, or do you just follow the lazy no-pruning precept, which allows the bushes to take up more and more space and to contain more and more useless dead wood? To my way of thinking, all roses need pruning every year. If, with the sweet briar, you prune out all the branches that have fruited, and leave in, untouched, all the young, unbranched shoots that have yet to perform in the next season (given adequate soil conditions) not only will it fruit abundantly but its young shoots will continue their extension right through the growing season, and it is these that waft the strongest fragrance.

So. Some roses are worth struggling for, after all.

Rosa 'Variegata di Bologna'

ANTHONY NOEL

'Variegata di Bologna'

❧

For such a famous and beautiful rose, very little is actually known about the origins of 'Variegata di Bologna.' The bare fact is that it was bred by a Signor A. Bonfiglioli at Garisenda around 1909. On the parentage of the rose, the identity of Signor Bonfiglioli, or what he thought about his remarkable creation, history has chosen to be silent. We must assume, however, that he was thrilled. For subsequent generations have been, and 'Variegata di Bologna,' for all its occasional crankiness and wayward habits, has proved a great favorite among gardeners, many of whom consider it to be the best of all striped roses.

Foliage, though it does not count for everything in a rose, still matters, and the leaves of 'Variegata di Bologna' are a fresh mid-green, neat and pointed, best always when grown in an enriched soil. That they are a little prone to black spot is indeed to be regretted, but nobody is perfect, and that is one more reason to keep the soil as fertile as possible. But what makes this rose unique is its generously produced flowers, about two inches in diameter, engagingly cupped like bowls, with irregular, black-currant stripes on a creamy-pink ground. Peter Beales, in his landmark book *Roses*, found the combination almost edible, like swirls of jam on semolina. 'Variegata di Bologna' is classed among the Bourbons, and, like most of them, it is deliciously fragrant. It flowers in mid- to late June, but—like wisteria—puts forth a modest second flush in late summer.

'Variegata di Bologna' is particularly greedy. It likes a deep, rich soil and a cool root run. Vita Sackville-West said that the plant did not grow very well for her, and Graham Stuart Thomas recommends growing the rose 'Variegata' against a northwest-facing wall. Certainly, the best specimen I have ever seen was in the rose garden he created at Monisfont Abbey, where 'Variegata di Bologna' reaches the very top of an old apple tree between eight and ten feet high, extravagantly throwing out its long rods of blossom in every direction.

Subsequently, I planted 'Variegata di Bologna' in my own garden, where at first it looked miserable, with leaves full of black spot. I started dribbling the hose on its roots for long periods, and applying generous doses of water-soluble tomato food, in that order. After a few weeks a miracle occurred, and my poor specimen started to grow like wildfire. Not having room for an apple tree in my small city patch, I trained its angular limbs on a trellis pyramid painted that curious, washed-out turquoise-gray one sometimes sees on old French chairs. The results, when it did finally come into bloom, were stunning.

Like all roses, 'Variegata di Bologna' enjoys clay soils, and is also a good candidate for city gardens. It is still important to apply a healthy mulch of well-rotted manure as soon as growth starts in the spring, as its appetite for that seems boundless. You must not, however, allow this mulch to touch the branches (as I am ashamed to say I did, before I knew better), for that will burn them, or indeed any plant. Merely tuck a comforting blanket over the surrounding soil, leaving the center free for old stems and new shoots to emerge.

If you grow 'Variegata di Bologna' as a free-standing shrub in, say, an old orchard (what a delightful idea!), be sure to keep the center nice and open, so that air passes through and light falls inside. That will go a great way toward keeping the bush free of black spot and other leaf diseases that thrive in close, congested conditions. Shorten the longest stems by about a third, to keep nice proportions and to minimize wind rock, which troubles the roots and may even cause the whole bush to snap off in a gale. Alternately, if you have a fine masonry wall (preferably northwest-facing, as Graham Stuart Thomas recommends), 'Variegata di Bologna' would be excellent trained there, and can reach as high as you might wish it to go. Lacking both orchard and wall, you might employ a trellis pyramid, as I have done, though it should be generous enough to make the bush comfortable—which is to say, at least eight feet tall and four feet across.

Finally, if you have access to hazel twigs (coppicing them from your own or a friend's bushes), then you are able to train 'Variegata di Bologna' in the nicest way of all—on a wigwam of bent hazel branches. (Young wood is best because it will not snap when bent into an arc.) Most old-fashioned and shrub roses will tend to produce their flowers at the tips of their branches, which often means that one's chief reasons for growing a rose—its flowers—are waving high overhead. But if tied horizontally they will produce flowers close at hand and the greater will be your floraison.

To be frank, no rose is particularly fine as a structure plant, and it may be that 'Variegata di Bologna' ranks low among what is, even from the start, an undistinguished crowd. The glory of old roses is their flowers, not their form. But all skilled garden work brings its own satisfaction, and so, if you have staked and tied in your 'Variegata di Bologna,' its thorny twigs will give you the sense of a job well done all winter, and the anticipation of glorious results in midsummer.

So why not attempt to exquisitely basket weave this rose over twigs, as they do at Sissinghurst? Make a sort of Folly out of the work itself. You have nothing to lose, and maybe everything to gain. For, among the most celebrated of the antique and shrub roses, none repays this sort of attention more than 'Variegata di Bologna,' which is magnificent—with some help.

Rosa 'Corylus'

PETER SCHNEIDER

'Corylus'

S OMEONE HAS CALCULATED that crossing any modern rose with any other modern rose will produce one of seventeen million possible results. Such is the jumble of genetics that makes up hybrid-tea and the modern shrub roses. And one is left wondering, then, why so many new roses look so much alike. But *Rosa* 'Corylus' is a much simpler affair, being a straightforward cross between the stalwart *Rosa rugosa* of northeastern Asia and *R. nitida*, a dwarf species native to eastern Canada and portions of New England.

'Corylus' inherits from *Rosa nitida* its delicate foliage and compact habit, and from *R. rugosa* height, impressive flower size, the signature crinkling of the leaves, and a long bloom period. Both *R. rugosa* and *R. nitida* can display brilliant autumn leaves, but 'Corylus' outdoes either of them, taking on almost every color of autumn and in doing so offering reason enough for growing it. Its flowers are silvery pink, about three and a half inches across, and single-petaled, with a brilliant boss of golden stamens and a spicy scent that carries on the wind. The flowers almost always arrive one to a stem, starting in early June in my northern-Ohio (USDA Zone 5b) garden, and appearing steadily for two or three weeks. The show will last longer in cool weather, though it can be dramatically abbreviated by heat. There is no repeat bloom, but the autumn foliage display persists for more than a month. Small, rounded hips begin turning orange as early as late July, and are bright red by September. I have never noticed birds sampling these fruits, but my birds may be spoiled by the plumper, juicier hips of the many other roses I grow. Individual blooms of 'Corylus' are too fleeting to make a satisfactory cut flower, but floral artists have found that it offers a great supply of attractive foliage.

When my wife, Susan, and I started turning a rolling hayfield into a series of gardens several years ago, we included 'Corylus' as one of the tough shrub roses in a hedge marking the edge of a hillside planting. In its first winter, the low temperature was minus 26 degrees Fahrenheit, and although for eight consecutive days the temperature never reached a high above zero, 'Corylus' came through without an inch of dieback. We have grown increasingly fond of it ever since. Our original plant is now five feet high and as wide, larger than it is reported to grow in England, its country of origin. Home from the hill and closer to the house, 'Corylus' contributes to the general floral abundance in June, while also acting, in a large perennial bed, as an unplanned but effective corral for the exuberant monarda called 'Marshall's Delight.' But our most effective and dramatic 'Corylus' combination to date has been alongside the steps to our deck, where it is placed in front of a *Heptacodium jasminoides* and behind a bank of *Coreopsis grandiflora* 'Early Sunrise.'

Lovely as its brief and delicate flowers are, 'Corylus' may be one of those roses that is most valued when it is out of bloom. Its shiny, feathery leaves remain healthy throughout the year, providing an effective counterpoint to broad, flat-leaved plants such as rhododendrons. 'Corylus' appreciates a little shelter, not for hardiness but for its fragile flowers, and, like many once-blooming, single-petaled roses, it is entirely happy in the high shade of deciduous trees. The dramatic progression of its autumn foliage from gold to orange to fiery red provides a mantle of maplelike color almost anywhere, without the invasive maple roots. In a mild climate, 'Corylus' may hold its foliage throughout the winter, but after severe frosts, when it is stripped of its leaves, it still shows interesting flaked, cinnamon-brown stems.

Most hedge roses earn their reputation from the dangerous prickles that make them impenetrable to man or beast. 'Corylus' serves as a great hedge plant simply because of its dense, many-caned growth. Its soft, almost furry bristles make it painless to work around, and if suckers are a problem, they can easily be controlled by cutting them close to the ground, or by using budded rather than own-root plants. Unlike one of its parents, *Rosa rugosa*, 'Corylus' has no gangliness, and it ends the garden year with all its leaves. When you spray more than twelve hundred roses, it is nice to be able to skip a few, and this is one I can always skip.

'Corylus' thrives in any ordinarily good garden soil, with or without extra fertilizer. A good supply of water throughout the summer intensifies the autumn foliage display. When used in foundation plantings or in any part of the garden where space is at a premium, 'Corylus' can easily be pruned to the desired shape or limits. Pruning immediately after bloom of course eliminates the show of hips, but it will not sacrifice the following year's flowers. Better, perhaps, to plant 'Corylus' where it has free space to develop all its most attractive characteristics of bush, bloom, foliage, and fruit.

'Corylus' is the creation of the great British rosarian and writer Hazel Le-Rougetel. It was she who did much to demystify the introduction of China and tea roses into the West, and to restore deserved credit to Ann Bentall, gardener to the great hybridizer of musk roses, the Reverend Joseph Pemberton. Earlier authorities assumed that Bentall, since she was working-class and female, merely introduced Pemberton's leftover creations after his death. LeRougetel demonstrated that she was an important hybridizer of roses in her own right.

'Corylus' is Hazel LeRougetel's single rose creation, and she named it after her own first name, *corylus* being the Latin genus name for the hazel. Some references rearrange the parentage of 'Corylus,' but in her own book, *A Heritage of Roses*, LeRougetel writes that *Rosa nitida* was the seed parent and *R. rugosa* provided the pollen. Normally, a cross between two true species will result in identical offspring, time after time. But because there is so much naturally occurring variability in *Rosa rugosa*, those who repeat LeRougetel's original cross may end up with a population of siblings with notable differences among them. That might be an interesting experiment. Still, it would be hard to find one better than 'Corylus.'

Rosa chinensis 'Mutabilis'

RORY DUSOIR

Rosa chinensis *'Mutabilis'*

PLANTS AND GARDENING took possession of me quietly, while I was an undergraduate studying classics at Balliol College, Oxford. Before that time, I don't recall showing any interest in gardening whatsoever. My mother used to teach us the names of common wildflowers on coastal walks when I was a child—primroses, sea pinks, campion. I forgot them every time.

I used to walk to college through a rough bit of pasture by the side of the Thames. Dog roses had formed huge mounds and banks, and overhung the river with the willows and alders. Walking there day after day, I began at last to take an interest in what was going on around me. I observed the unfolding minutiae of the humdrum local vegetation, surprised by each tiny floral event. Dead nettles and ground ivy were a revelation. Apple trees stunned me with their blossoms. But the abiding image in my mind is of the roses in full hip, cascading down to the water, lit up in winter by the fine, dying light. As the year grew ever colder, the rose hips burned with an even greater warmth. The virgin, unbranched shoots—growth of the preceding season—described huge bristling arcs above, each an expression of raw, youthful vigor.

So—roses became my first enthusiasm. And no flower was better created to appeal to my attenuated imagination, accustomed as it was to casting into the largely forgotten, poorly documented, mysterious depths of early history, reading damaged texts, and constructing hypotheses stretched thin to bridge yawning gaps in our fragmented, clutched-at knowledge of the classical period. The mystery of it all appealed to me at the time. Our efforts appeared so doomed to failure, the evidence filtered through generations of similarly hapless, scribbling monks, always raising more questions than were answered. We always ended up following leads to the same point of pure conjecture, faced in the end with a historical silence.

A similar mystery unshakably attends our study of the rose, a plant whose cultivation has roots deep in the prehistory of so many cultures. Tracing the convoluted lineage of almost any rose leads us through different ages, cultures, and continents to the inevitable point where we are looking back into the unknown. *Rosa gallica* var. 'Officinalis,' *Rosa centifolia*, *Rosa damascena*, *Rosa alba*, and *Rosa chinensis* are all varieties or complex hybrids derived from ancient, uncharted cultivation, their parents long forgotten. And it thrilled me that they were still living things, these relics. You could smell and touch them, the same roses that had descended through centuries and millennia, donating pollen at every turn to the vast, intricate web of rose genealogy. They possessed a breathing immediacy that scraps of literature and broken pots lacked.

In the end, this excitement of immediate experience, of working directly with plants, wrested me away from academic study and into full-time gardening. My early romantic enthusiasm for roses has since, as a result, waned ungratefully— tempered in cruel fashion by the prosaic, practical constraints that, I'm sad to say, attend the business of creating a beautiful garden. Two years of working under Christopher Lloyd at Great Dixter, in particular, have instilled in me a certain skepticism toward the genus. For, here, sentiment and association have little power to influence planting. The performance of a plant is all that matters in a garden where visual effect, maintained over a long season, is the first priority. A rose like *R. setipoda* wins its place more for the effect of its vigorous, arching structure and markedly flagon-shaped hips than for its fleeting floral performance. So does *R. virginiana* because it has such excellent year-round appeal, marking each season with a fresh display, whether of blossom, branch, hip, or foliage. Some members of the superb hybrid-musk group also make the grade. Their foliage and structure create a solid enough background, but it is their exceptionally long and fragrant blooming that makes them worthwhile.

There is, however, no special place at Dixter for roses. Each plant is judged solely on its practical merits. Fancy names in French and Latin cannot redeem a disease-prone plant with nothing more to offer than a flowering season of three weeks. No matter if 'Cuisse de Nymphe,' 'Ispahan,' and *Rosa mundi* suggest to you, with all the weight of historical association, pictures of earthly delight. In a wet June, your collection of old roses will be a sodden, diseased mess, a paradise only for the rotten fungi that gorge themselves on the fragrant, thickly petaled blossoms and turn them into a horrific brown slime:

> *O Rose, thou art sick!*
> *The invisible worm*
> *That flies in the night,*
> *In the howling storm,*
> *Has found out thy bed*
> *Of crimson joy:*
> *And his dark secret love*
> *Doth thy life destroy.*
> —WILLIAM BLAKE,
> "The Sick Rose" (1794)

Fatalists will accept this tragedy stoically time and time again, reminding themselves of the year before last, when the roses were magnificent. But a practical person will eventually be forced to admit defeat and plant something better.

Once I had discovered my ambition to become a gardener, Oxford was a splendid place to be. It is quite a green town. The Rivers Thames and Cherwell wind through it, their banks and pastures protected from development by the colleges that own them. But much more lies within the college buildings themselves. They dominate the town center on all sides, showing an austere front to the outside world. The layout reflects a long history of hostility—sometimes violent—between the ordinary residents of the town and the members of the university, who felt obliged to protect their privileged existence behind tall, forbidding walls. This tradition of hostility is still proudly maintained, as you would expect. Many of the colleges retain a fortresslike appearance and mentality, and visits by the general public, whether local residents or not, are zealously restricted by the porters who guard the gates of every college. But a student of the university has the run of the place, a fact of which I took full advantage.

The colleges of Oxford and Cambridge were originally monastic institutions, and are the sole present-day representatives of the incredibly rich monastic tradition that existed in medieval Britain. The monks were wiped out by Henry VIII's zealous reformation of the Church of England. But as academic institutions, the Oxbridge colleges survived, and their gardens still exemplify the medieval ideal of a *hortus conclusus*—a hidden, tranquil place shut off from the noise, bustle, and stench of the outside world. The walls that surround them were intended as much to nurture the education of the occupants in quiet contemplation as to provide shelter for the plants that were grown there. I spent a great deal of time frequenting these gardens at this exciting early stage of my infatuation with plants. Although the result could hardly have been foreseen, they did a great deal to nurture my budding horticultural ambition.

My own college, Balliol, had a comparatively small garden, but it contained two or three plants that stick in my memory. Among them was a rose, *Rosa chinensis* 'Mutabilis,' which grew at the base of one of the limestone walls of the college. In that privileged, south-facing, sheltered position, the shrub grew to dimensions of which it is not capable in more exposed gardens in this country. It was the largest rosebush I have ever seen, seven feet high and as wide. It produced a mass of blossoms, and it is in their masses that these flowers are best appreciated—for they are flimsy things, loose single petals of silk, commonly compared to butterflies. And as such, they swarm all over this shrub in their different colors, pointed flames of orange buds opening to a soft yellow that matures by degrees to deep crimson, after which the petals fall and die. The conceit is that pollination triggers the change of color, as though the flowers blush at their fecundation. Each flower lasts three days, but they are produced in an endless sequence. All the different color stages populate the plant in their hundreds from June into early November, or as long as the weather is mild.

Not much is known of the history of this rose. It was introduced to Europe around 1900. Before that, there is only silence; we can only guess at its age and history of cultivation in its native China. It may reach back through centuries. But my fondness for that rose can only grow, bound up as it is in that formative time and place in my life. Roses were central to my early horticultural awakening, and Oxford was central. And here is a rose whose image cannot be blighted by succeeding memories of brown dead heads and dieback, whose petals mature and die gracefully. It occupies a special place in my mind, nurtured in the lee of those protective walls, redolent of ancient history and new beginnings.

Rosa 'Graham Thomas'

DAVID WHEELER

'Graham Thomas'

HEREFORDSHIRE, mid–October: overnight, seemingly, a rare Indian summer turns into an English winter. Gone the high blue skies and hours of earth-warming sun; gone the smell of bruised fruit strewn uneaten over orchard grass; gone, too, the dry seedheads so beloved of goldfinches; and gone the dew-spangled cobwebs, hanging sodden now from every twig and bough. In their place fog and rain, pewter clouds clamped to the roof of the house; it is cold, and a seeping dampness permeates the greenhouse, the potting shed, the loggia, the entire garden. Yesterday's brittle autumn leaves are today's sludge. Fish in the ornamental ponds have gone deep.

But this is England, hard against the Welsh border, where Bryan's Ground occupies a few acres surrounded by low hills and broadleaf woods. We're used to these fickle weather patterns at this time of year (at all times of the year!), and many of our plants have also cottoned on. Unless there is a killing frost, or a week of gales and hard-driven icy rain, the garden will resurrect itself briefly and, like the diva who has yet to sing her last notes, let loose its grand finale. Part of this closing cavalcade is the roses.

Our garden is filled with roses: species roses, climbing roses, rambling roses, shrub roses, old-fashioned roses, new roses, healthy roses, and diseased roses. And if I want to pick fresh blooms for the house this autumn day, I go straight to the part of the garden where some of David Austin's English roses are gathered together in a box-edged parterre. Few rose breeders of recent years have given us such plentiful treasure as David Austin, some of his creations rivaling the splendor to be found in the aristocratic-sounding ranks of nineteenth-century French varieties. Who would be without his 'Constance Spry'? Who would snub his 'Gertrude Jekyll'? Also riding high in Austin's catalogue is 'Graham Thomas,' hardy and unusually floriferous. Who, then, is the man for whom this hearty rose is named?

I first met Graham Thomas in the early 1990s in his own garden, having been asked to write a profile of him for the American magazine *Horticulture*. It was January, but despite the year's low ebb, his suburban Surrey plot—just a few miles from the Royal Horticultural Society's garden at Wisley—sparkled like a tray of jewels. Beneath sweetly scented mahonia ('Underway,' and 'Lionel Fortescue'), perfumed viburnums and sarcococca grew heathers, early crocuses, and hellebores. Daffodils were beginning to break bud, and within a few weeks there would be blooms of what Thomas calls "the best of the big-flowered rhododendrons," 'Nobleanum Venustum.'

Graham Stuart Thomas can fairly be reckoned the twentieth century's father of English gardening. Born in 1909, he began his unpaid working life at the Cambridge University Botanic Garden soon after leaving school at the age of sixteen. After two and a half years, he decided it was time to start earning some money and went to work for Clarence Elliot, who grew some two hundred thousand alpines at the famous Six Hills Nursery. In 1932, Thomas moved to Hillings, wholesale growers specializing in coniferous and broadleaf trees, shrubs, roses, rhododendrons, climbers, and herbaceous perennials.

In the exigencies of World War II, the 330 acres at Hillings were turned over to cereal and vegetable production, and after the war the old working practices— "the days of spades and horses," as Graham describes them—slipped into the past. Thomas moved on again, forming a partnership with his friend James Russell to help run the down-at-the-heels but well-known Sunningdale Nursery. Russell and Thomas positioned themselves at the forefront of England's postwar horticultural scene, and began to introduce their prize-winning roses, azaleas, and rhododendrons to a wider public at the annual Chelsea Flower Show. Private commissions soon came Thomas's way, including a request from Her Majesty the Queen Mother to design new plantings for her garden at Royal Lodge.

By this time, Graham Thomas had also started to write, bringing out in 1957 *The Old Shrub Roses*, first in a long and distinguished sequence of books about gardens, roses, and other plants. He had also been appointed part-time adviser to the National Trust, with a watching brief over such important gardens as Blickling Hall in Norfolk, Cotehele in Cornwall, Sheffield Park in Sussex, Polesden Lacey in Surrey, Killerton in Devon, Stourhead in Wiltshire, and, most famous of them all, perhaps, Hidcote Manor in Gloucestershire, where Lawrence Johnston, an American born in Paris, had made one of England's finest gardens.

Today, the National Trust's *Handbook* lists more than a hundred gardens open to the public, and closest to Thomas's own heart is Mottisfont Abbey in Hampshire. Here, over old brick walls and in gravelly, chalky soil beside the River Test, he has deposited his unsurpassed collection of old roses in a garden of his own design. He views Mottisfont as an extension of his own garden in a sense, and although he no longer often makes the hundred-mile round trip to see "his" roses, there is no doubt that they are mulched with his greatest affection.

Thus it was that roses became synonymous with the name Graham Thomas, and thus it became inevitable that one day he would be asked to give his name to a new variety.

I asked how it came about. "David Austin said he would like to name a rose after me, and would I choose one. I was confronted [at Austin's nursery near Wolverhampton] by a whole field of approved seedlings, on trial, six of a sort. They were all from white through blush, pink, etcetera, a few reds, and *one* yellow, the first he had raised of this colour. And I chose it."

Austin told me he bred the mostly repeat-flowering and sweetly scented English roses in a quest to develop "a delicacy of appearance that is often lacking in so many of the roses of our time; to catch something of that unique charm which we associate with old roses." And of 'Graham Thomas,' then his only yellow, he said, "It is one of the best English roses up to the present time." With a hint of apricot in the early stages, "it has flowers of the richest and purest deep-yellow colouring, a shade which would be difficult to match in any other rose, certainly in any other shrub rose." Raised in 1983, it is the result of a cross between another English rose, 'Charles Austin' (bred in 1973), and an earlier Austin cross that had as a parent the renowned white-flowered 'Iceberg.' "I had hoped for yellow seedlings," says Austin, "but did not expect a color of such intensity."

'Graham Thomas' has cup-shaped flowers ("chaliced at first," says David Austin) three to four inches across, the petals "mingling loosely within" and bunched in the manner of floribundas, occasionally throwing an unusually large bloom at the center of the spray. With glossy, dark-green foliage and relatively few thorns, it can hardly be bettered.

At Bryan's Ground we grow 'Graham Thomas' in association with roses of a similar or closely related hue ('Buff Beauty,' 'Mrs Oakley Fisher,' and Austin's 'Windrush'), underplanted with dusty-blue catnip (*Nepeta*). Common fennel thrusts upward through the bushes as summer advances, its pungent scent blending exotically with the strong tea-rose fragrance of 'Graham Thomas.'

So—any faults? "Well," says Graham with some amusement, "it was turned down at one garden for being too lanky." Garden designers make the most of this idiosyncrasy, however, and place it in mixed borders where roses of a lax or spreading habit might smother neighboring plants. 'Graham Thomas' is said to grow to a height of about four feet, but reports of much larger specimens, always taller than wide, prevail. It grows in the Yellow Border at Kiftsgate Court, opposite Hidcote Manor in Gloucestershire. "Such a good rose," says Anne Chambers, whose grandmother began the Kiftsgate garden—famous for another rose—between the two world wars. "No disease and not too hard a yellow. My only problem with it is its growth: however hard I prune it, it still reaches ten feet, so it is quite difficult to stake, as it also flowers so heavily. Right now [early

October] it is looking lovely, with masses of flowers." Gardeners from as far afield as South Africa and California say much the same.

'Graham Thomas' the rose is a late adolescent; Graham Thomas the rosarian is approaching his centenary. If the one abides as long as the other, gardeners will indeed have much to celebrate.

David Wheeler's essay was written a few weeks before Graham Thomas's death on 16 April 2003, aged ninety-four.

Rosa richardii

MIRABEL OSLER

Rosa sancta

Oh, no man knows
Through what wild centuries
Roves back the rose.

—WALTER DE LA MARE,
"All That's Past" (1912)

WHEN I FIRST BEGAN WITH ROSES, moving into that vast territory of scent, form, and color, I knew nothing. I was simply a garden ignoramus. So whatever made me plant this one, my first? Why this rose? Was it instinct? It could certainly not have been sagacity. But does it really matter, when some of the best things we grow in our gardens are fortuitous rather than wise? In any case, my rose is one that travels by many beautiful names: *Rosa sancta, Rosa richardii*, the Holy Rose of Abyssinia. I planted it in a wild setting among unkempt grass. There, it blossomed against a background of alders growing along the banks of a stream haunted by dippers and kingfishers.

The first time I saw this rose in flower was from our bedroom window. It was early one June morning when, drawn like an involuntary sleepwalker, I walked across the grass, leaving footprints in the dew. Transfixed, astonished to see the results of what we had planted, I put out my hand. (For isn't touch as important to gardening as sight and scent?) The foliage was dark, the buds were bright pink, the five-petaled flowers were flushed as apple blossoms, flawless as quince, with a cluster of brilliant stamens that shuddered at the touch. Knowing its venerable pedigree, seeing its sprawling deportment and its disheveled petals with a life more transitory than that of a butterfly, I knew then that no dawn could be squandered while this rose was in bloom.

That morning many years ago was memorable for my discovery that something ticked in a catalogue turned out to be a winner. And later, in autumn, when the bush was covered with shiny small hips, their blackness a contrast to the more usual orange and red on other roses, the understated color, latent and curious, seemed fitting for a rose with such an ancient genealogy. For, according to Dr. C. C. Hurst (1870–1947), a pioneer on the heredity of roses, *Rosa richardii*, discovered growing in the courtyards of Abyssinian temples, may have been longer in cultivation than any other rose.

Graham Stuart Thomas, writing on the history of the Holy Rose in his book *The Old Shrub Roses*, opened windows of the mind far beyond my shortsighted expectations, bedded down merely in bone meal and mulch. Imagine! My rose, bought on impulse, may have originated with a saint. For Mr. Thomas writes that "St Frumentius was born in Phoenicia about A.D. 300." Captured by Ethiopians, the saint was taken to the Abyssinian capital, where, as the King's secretary, he is said "to have converted the Abyssinians to Christianity." Thus, the rose may well have been found "within the precincts of the Christian churches." I have read still further of the legendary ancestry loaded upon this rose. Sacred to the celebrated Egyptian goddess Isis, it was identified as the variety petrified in a wreath unearthed by the archaeologist Flinders Petrie in a tomb at Hawara, in Lower Egypt. *Rosa sancta* was also depicted on Cretan frescoes during the Minoan period. Later, early Christians perceived the five petals to represent the five wounds of Christ. The mind rocks to facts that ignite one's imagination. So much history, so many years of human experience, carried by a rose that grew in our orchard in the Welsh Marches.

I know there are other roses with the same frailty as *Rosa sancta*. The scented *R. alba* 'Semi-plena,' for instance, smelling of mock orange; or *R. carolina*, the Dunwich rose; or 'Frühlingsanfang' and 'Frülingsmorgen,' which formed a scented hedge seen distantly through our apple trees. Among singles, there are the silvery-pink *Rosa gallica* 'Complicata' and *R. macrantha*, with its pristine white, yellow-stamened flowers, and the early-blooming ferny-leafed *R. hugonis*, with its clear, primrose-yellow blossoms. And there is the feral dog rose, *Rosa canina*, which festoons the hedges in summer. Each one possesses blooms of varying degrees of fragility, but also of great beauty. And I would give anything to grow the magnificent climber 'Cooper's Burmese' (*R. laevigata cooperi)*, with large, single white flowers looking brittle as porcelain. Alas, it is too tender for the town garden where I now live.

Planting the wrong rose in the wrong place is almost endemic to gardening. We wasted several seasons before facing unavoidable reality, for no manual warned us of the maddening diversity of roses. No horticultural expert pointed to the characteristics, variable habits, and seemingly willful behavior of roses. Certainly color, scent, and size are listed in catalogues, but when I was floundering among choices and confusing nomenclature, no kind friend took me by the hand and said, "Beware of that noncompliant climber—it won't cover your arbor, nor will it embroider that boring evergreen you regret having bought." So I planted those of sturdy stance where I required pliancy, thrusters where I needed droopers, or barbaric bulwarks, perfect for withstanding gales and intruding cattle, where I really wanted roses to cascade and drape in trees and over walls. Thus, many summers were frittered away through a lack of know-how.

My chosen rose is quite the opposite of the frenetic sort, the kind that seems to smolder with inflamed color. But, as with so many other things in life and gardening, there's usually a snag in one's object of desire. Rust, black spot, mildew, mold, and so forth are well-known banes of roses. Yet the most common accusation visitors made against the collection of old roses my husband and I assembled was their nonrecurrent flowering. *Rosa × richardii* is one of the worst. Its flowers are brief, fleeting, ephemeral as sunset, or spume blown across the sea. The rose is over before there's time for a second look. And the sanguine gardener who foolishly goes for a holiday may miss a whole year's performance. With us it was mid-June when it bloomed, and by the second week of July—if gales and rain hadn't already battered the petals—the show was over. But that's fine. The late Henry Mitchell in his wonderful book *The Essential Earthman* lists among his ideal demands a rose that has "constancy of bloom." I don't. Nor do I demand snake's-head fritillaries, windflowers, or snowdrops that bloom from spring well into autumn. Mitchell is against *alba*s because, "Who wants a rose that does not bloom on and off all summer and fall?" I do, Henry, *I* do! Goodness! Imagine the tedium of daffodils switching on and off for months on end! However, I forgive his wholesale condemnation when I read that he loves the fragrant 'Sarah van Fleet.' This superb *rugosa*, with its pinkness, fragrance, and annual fidelity, once lifted a corner of our country garden every summer that we were there.

Vita Sackville-West grew *Rosa sancta* at Sissinghurst, yet it is unusual to find more than a passing reference to it in gardening books. Many other roses have high profiles, with their noble names and detailed descriptions, both of which are often irresistibly romantic, and often misleading. I find the gush I write about some of these aristocratic beauties sticks to my fingers like petunia petals, until I see a row of 'Alpine Sunset' against a California backdrop of bosky undulation stretching almost to Tennessee. Then the ink in my pen turns acid. But whatever fads and fashions ebb and flow in the world of smart gardening, I come down every time on the side of the antique shrub roses, the *gallica*s, *centifolia*s, damasks, *alba*s. They may be old hat, but as far as my emotions are concerned, I am stuck with them. When bamboos, gravel, and grasses became trendy and turned garden conformity on its head, they did nothing to tingle my libido. But the sight of 'Variegata di Bologna' across the sward in Katherine Swift's sequence of historical gardens in Shropshire made me sigh with longing for the heyday of the garden my husband and I made on the Welsh Marches, where the scent of old roses saturated the atmosphere.

Having written this piece on a rose that has been a favorite and has claimed more constancy than my usual fickleness over other plants, I have just discovered an opposing way of looking, which turns all my rosy assumptions inside out. It seems that, for two poets, my Holy Rose of Abyssinia—with its quality of sweetness and innocence rather than sensuality—expresses something else altogether. A friend recently gave me a copy of *Tender Taxes: Versions of Rilke's French Poems*, in which the poet Jo Shapcott feels compelled to respond to the German poet's erotic imagery in his twenty-one lyrics on chosen roses. Her answer to Rilke's poem "Rosa sancta" ends with these menacing words (no doubt to be spoken *sub rosa*): "I stink of the Fall."

That fairly knocks on the head my subjective view of this rose. Such, I suppose, is the power of poetry that I shall never again tiptoe through the dew with the same primary vision I possessed on my first sighting of *Rosa sancta, Rosa richardii*, the Holy Rose of Abyssinia.

Rosa pimpinellifolia 'Double White'

PAGE DICKEY

Rosa pimpinellifolia *'Double White'*

A<small>FTER FORTY YEARS</small> of impassioned gardening and the accompanying mania for collecting all kinds of perennials, biennials, and shrubs, I find, curiously, that it is not the new, exotic flower that sends a thrill down my spine but, rather, certain centuries-old garden favorites. Snowdrops do it to me in March, and drifts of daffodils—the small-cupped sorts and muddled old doubles—in April. Carpets of pale primroses can make me swoon, as well as a fat clump of ragged-edged, spicy-smelling pinks, or a drift of spotted foxgloves. White Japanese anemones, fragile jewels on willowy stems, prompt sighs of delight in autumn. But nothing makes me as weak in the knees as the sight and smell of a rose.

Oh, not any rose. I am left unmoved by hybrid teas and floribundas, though their colors are luscious. I can intellectually appreciate all the new shrub roses, the ones hybridized in Northern climes for extreme hardiness that are useful for landscaping, but I don't shiver with pleasure at the sight of them. No, the roses that I love are the very old sorts, the swirled doubles and pure singles that weigh down graceful bushes and bowl you over with their fragrance. The Burnet roses, varieties of *Rosa pimpinellifolia* (also called *R. spinosissima*), are perfect examples. Blooming in masses on small, bristly, fern-leaved shrubs, they range from simple single-petaled forms with golden stamens, to semi-double and double, in cream white, blush, pink, or butter yellow—all intensely, deliciously scented.

Needless to say, the ancient *alba*s, damasks, *gallicas*, and *centifolia*s offer countless varieties that are the epitome of gorgeous rose beauty and perfume, and I would not be without them in the garden. But by summer's end these ravishing roses are indeed ravished—by Japanese beetles and black spot; and unless you spray with hideous poisons, you end up with pathetic skeletons by fall. So I find I turn more and more to the rugged species roses and their close hybrids that keep their foliage healthy and tidy all summer, and yet supply the look and scent I crave. Many of the *rugosa*s satisfy—'Blanc Double de Coubert,' 'Sarah van Fleet,' 'Agnes,' and 'Roseraie de l'Haÿ,' for instance—and the early *hugonis* sorts, like *R.* 'Cantabrigiensis,' with its tall arching branches of sweet-scented, cream-yellow single flowers and fernlike foliage. But the Burnet roses are also exemplary; and two of the kinds my husband and I grow in our North Salem, New York, garden—the single white and the double—have an unpretentious charm that bowls me over. In fact, the 'Double White' is, hands down, my favorite early-blooming rose.

Many double forms of *R. pimpinellifolia* exist, but their names have sometimes been lost, resulting in the simplicity of naming them "double white" or "double pink." Mary McMurtrie, the Scottish watercolorist and plantsman, now in her nineties, is an expert on these roses. The Burnet species have a wide natural distribution throughout Europe, thriving in the poor sandy soils of coastlines, but they were hybridized extensively in Scotland in the nineteenth century. Their popularity declined with the advent of the gaudy, repeat-blooming roses of the twentieth century, but favorite varieties were handed on, nameless, from gardener to gardener. Mrs. McMurtrie writes in her lovely book, *Scots Roses*, of several different forms of the 'Double White,' as well as double pinks and yellows, and slight variations on the single-white species. Even our best rose catalogues seem confused over the names of the Burnets. But the good news is: You can't go wrong. They are all entrancing.

The single and the double Burnets are the very first roses to bloom in our garden at Duck Hill. The single Burnet is the smallest-growing rose we have—perhaps the true species—with arching stems to two feet, clothed with fine-textured, intricately cut foliage. Overnight in May it becomes a mass of scented cream-white flowers. Our graceful, fine-textured clump of the 'Double White,' which is a foot or two taller, stands by an old gatepost; by mid-May it, too, is smothered in blossoms—small, swirled, globular white flowers that reveal a hint of golden stamens. They exude a fragrance that Graham Stuart Thomas writes is half their charm—fresh and exhilarating, "like lily of the valley in its revivifying purity."

These are roses that are handed along from friend to friend, not only because they are treasures, but because, if they are grown on their own roots (rather than grafted), they run by stolons to form a thicket, sometimes traveling farther than you had intended. Consequently, there are always rooted suckers to give away.

But allow the Burnets room to spread, for their thicketlike growth results in an effective mass in the landscape. The delicately cut leaves of these roses stay fresh all summer, unnoticed by Japanese beetles, and turn tawny red-green colors in autumn. The flowers are followed in late summer by round maroon-black hips, often compared to large black currants. Even in winter, the roses are appealing because of their rust-brown bristly stems. Gertrude Jekyll writes in her book on roses: "These fine hardy Briers have also one merit that most roses lack, for in winter the leafless crowd of close-growing, plentifully-prickled branches forms masses of warm bronze colouring that have quite a comforting appearance. The pretty Briers might well replace the dull and generally ugly steep slopes of turf that disfigure so many gardens. They are charming accompaniments to steps and their low balustrades; they are equally in place in the humblest garden and the most exalted, and in all sorts and kinds of places and for all kinds of uses they hardly ever come amiss."

Rosa 'Veilchenblau'

MAC GRISWOLD

'Veilchenblau'

I FIRST SAW THE RAMBLING ROSE 'Veilchenblau' ten years ago—an enormous blob of purple sunning itself on a shed roof in the outskirts of Sag Harbor, on Long Island. I recall the shed as being covered with tarpaper— granted it was painted a handsome dark green, but it was still tarpaper. Could this really be true, I wonder? The choice of siding seems preposterous, given that this place belonged to a successful Manhattan art dealer. Her house was being substantially renovated, and an elaborate garden was being designed for her. There may, however, be some truth to this story. Before the place was transformed, the shed had been more of a shack, a shabby garage that opened onto a hardtop driveway, the kind that sometimes gets called a "working driveway"—meaning the car gets jacked up there when it needs work and sometimes stays there for quite a long time. The tarpaper stage might have been a way station along the path to perfection. In any case, what I remember besides the blast of purple was how the warm air was filled with the tonic and medicinal scent of tarpaper, an ineffable, down-at-heel fragrance. Tarpaper can smell of poverty, can be the reminder of Walker Evans's sharecroppers, but for me it conjures up childhood secrecy and independence. My "playhouse" as a child was an old chicken house—tarpaper, of course—moved away from the other, still–chicken-filled chicken houses into a distant thicket, set on cinderblocks, whitewashed inside, and given to me as a birthday present.

But back to the rose. Maybe the tarpaper perfume took over because 'Veilchenblau' has so little fragrance? Graham Stuart Thomas, in *The Rose Book*, insists that it smells like green apples; Peter Beales, in *Classic Roses*, calls it "moderately fragrant." Who am I to disagree with these two magisters of the rose? Sniff as hard as I can, all I detect is what Thomas, describing another rose, calls "only an apology" for fragrance.

But whatever 'Veilchenblau' lacks in fragrance, or in length of bloom (it flowers once, early in June), doesn't matter to me. Soon after that initial sighting, I bought a house in Sag Harbor, too. The pleasurable thought of this raffish boudoir hue washing across the second story of my demure village dwelling more than made up for any other deficiency. When I ordered the first roses for the new garden, 'Veilchenblau' was one of them. Ten years later, it requires severe annual pruning to keep the view clear out the second-story bedroom windows. My rose has few thorns and clean, almost mildew-free, light-green foliage with long pointed leaves a little like a willow's. Its habit is as good as its color is shocking. It is willing to grow exuberantly high—eighteen feet, more than the twelve predicted by the rose pundits—on the northeast wall of the house where the nor'easters blow in the wintertime.

Climbers and ramblers are what botanists call "scramblers," writes Thomas, meaning they can't really hold on by themselves, though they can throw a hooked cane over a branch as a good start. Certainly they can't climb a house unaided. 'Veilchenblau' is a rambler, which means its growth is looser and laxer (untidier, some might say) than that of a climber, and therefore it is easier to bend and attach to any support. Its yearly ascent of my house has been marked by the addition of one horizontal trellis section above another, almost all the way up to the gable. The siding is clapboard, so special care has been taken, because even gardeners who love climbers must sometimes paint their houses. First, four short projecting supports are nailed to the wall. Then the new trellis is hung on them across the house front, and secured with hooks and eyes instead of nails. The idea is that, when the house needs paint, the trellises—with 'Veilchenblau' attached—can be unhooked and eased onto the painter's scaffolding. So far, although the house is scabby with peeling paint and I have talked a lot about the inventive scheme, I somehow haven't had the nerve to try it out with this rose.

A dictator over more than painting schedules, 'Veilchenblau' has also managed to control the color of the house. This makes sense, since I coveted the imperious purple beauty even before I had the wall up which to grow it. Maybe I bought the house to grow the rose? That is probably partly true—certainly most gardeners don't buy houses where they can't imagine gardening. Whatever the sequence was, gray became the color. Long before house and rose came together, I had learned a good lesson about color for gardens and houses when I saw Winslow Homer's watercolors of Bermuda. Among the parakeet-colored houses that he painted is a gray one, gray with mauve shadows and sparks of red flowers in the foreground. I wanted a gray house less for its grayness than for what would show up against it. A white house turns every garden beneath it to mush, in my opinion.

"Violet-blue" is the translation of my favorite rose's name. But in fact no flowering violet approaches the variety of shades 'Veilchenblau' exhibits over its three-week bloom period. Crimson-purple buds open to a lavender-purple; then, as the fat trusses of small semi-double flowers begin to age, whatever red coloring exists fades away, until the effect is nearly blue. Finally, they turn lilac-gray, which may be the best transformation of all. Each little flower is flecked and striped with white.

'Veilchenblau' was hybridized in 1909, and a close look at its background does not reveal what you'd call a distinguished ancestry. Not very far back in the family tree is *Rosa multiflora*, a mid-nineteenth-century introduction from China with puffy, lacelike clusters of single white flowers. It was recognized early on in its Western career as a superb, reliably rooting parent and as a hardy understock for more tender roses. As a landscape plant, *Rosa multiflora* swept the East Coast's cattle and dairy regions sometime in the first half of the twentieth century, when it was distributed widely by state extension services as the answer to barbed wire.

However, when it began sprouting so wildly in the pastures that there was hardly room left for a cow to graze, and field mowers wrecked their mowing bars trying to cut it back, *R. multiflora* was abandoned as the government's favorite hedging plant. Still, it has an incredible fragrance. The giant hedges left over from that ill-fated experiment are now twined with another June-blooming and highly invasive exotic, Japanese honeysuckle, *Lonicera japonica*. When the two flower together, the blended perfume can knock you sideways. So how, you might ask, did 'Veilchenblau' end up with no smell?

Point the finger directly at one parent: 'The Engineer,' a.k.a. 'Turner's Crimson Rambler,' a *Rosa multiflora* cross that nonetheless is virtually scentless. 'The Engineer,' a bright but noncommittal red, a sort of 1950s Revlon lipstick red, was a real favorite when it first arrived from Japan. To create 'Veilchenblau,' 'The Engineer' was crossed in Germany by a Mr. Schmitt with a crimson-purple hybrid perpetual rose called 'Souvenir de Brod,' which had been hybridized in Hungary but was named after the Bosnian town we know all too well from the recent war. What borders does a rose hybrid not cross?

The first roses I knew were pink, white, red, yellow. All our roses were nameless. All were planted in places that told me they didn't count for much. It was a landscape that gave pride of place to flowering shrubs and trees, and where delphiniums, dahlias, and gladiolas (not yet irretrievably vulgar, though we worried about it) were grown in a cutting garden. The pink and white climbers grew in the kitchen courtyard against a pink-and-white brick wall; the scentless, bright-red ones—surely 'The Engineer'?—were splayed against a post-and-rail fence on the driveway, visible only as a carmine blur as the Buick moved smoothly in and out on the gravel. The "laundry rose," a pinkish-yellow shrub rose, spread itself out lavishly near the drying yard.

All the other first-comers to the Sag Harbor garden excepting 'Veilchenblau' were rational choices. I picked roses that love our sandy soil, like *Rosa* 'Nevada,' and roses I'd made notes on while visiting gardens during some long gardenless years spent in the city. When I began to garden again, it certainly never occurred to me to grow roses that had to do with my childhood. *Rosa banksiae* 'Lutea' is a memento of a lover in sunny Charleston in April, when the walls are heaped with the fluffy, creamy pillows of tiny flowers. Dark and gloomy Herefordshire Novembers with some of my oldest and best garden friends gave me *Rosa moyesii* 'Geranium,' dangling with coral fruits as long and lively as my best chandelier earrings.

'Veilchenblau' is part of the same bouquet of intentions that a gardener—with or without a garden—gathers in other people's gardens. But 'Veilchenblau' is somehow different, because, without meaning to do so at all, I had picked a rose with a link to my far-distant past. It is beautiful and vulgar, indecently purple, and outrageously like nothing I'd seen before—but it still smells like a tarpaper shack, like independence again, and at last.

'VEILCHENBLAU'

Rosa 'Betty Prior'

THOMAS C. COOPER

'Betty Prior'

⌒

THE ROSE 'Betty Prior' is rumored to be the favorite of the Queen of England, and if this is true, I imagine the appeal for her is similar to that of another English institution for which she has a well-documented affection—the sensible shoe. For, if she is nothing else, the Queen is sensible, and 'Betty Prior' is, in addition to her many other attributes, an extremely sensible rose. No rose betters her for length of blooming season—from very early summer to the beginnings of winter in my garden on the outskirts of Boston—or for indifference to pests, diseases, or batterings from wayward soccer balls and misguided sprinkler systems, to say nothing of general brown-thumbed ineptitude offered up by gardeners. She is not prone to the vapors when the weather takes a turn for the worse; her flowers are not so complicated or fragile that they collapse almost upon opening. Come what may, Ms. Prior produces blooms held above fresh, matte green leaves, providing colorful accompaniment for both the alliums of early summer and the bleached wands of ornamental grasses in early winter.

An upright bush three to five feet tall and roughly vase-shaped, 'Betty Prior' throws out dense sprays of two-and-a-half-inch single flowers whose petals fade from rich pink at their tips to pale pink at their bases, where they surround a modest circle of yellow stamens. The overall effect reminds some people of our native dogwood. Only a hint of fragrance reaches my nose, but others are more enthusiastic. In any event, the perfume is not powerful, for this is not an extravagant rose. She is Betty, not Elizabeth, but she is sturdy and hardy (to Zone 4) and beautiful in an understated fashion. So I join the Queen in honoring 'Betty Prior' as a favorite; and if that's not her opinion, it should be.

For many years, countless gardeners here and abroad also considered 'Betty Prior' a favorite. She is a modern rose, bred in an era long before today's urge to create flowers with the voluptuous good looks of the old cabbage sorts. 'Betty' is appropriately classed as a floribunda ("producing abundant flowers"), a generally ungainly group originally termed Poulsen roses, then hybrid *polyantha*s, then floribundas, and subsequently modern cluster-flowered bush roses—none a name likely to win an award for marketing savvy. 'Betty Prior' is very similar to the original Poulsen rose 'Else Poulsen,' but produces a slightly larger bloom in a softer shade of pink. All that aside, she does produce great clusters of flowers—though, because they are delicate singles, one never gets the impression that the plant is weighed down, literally or visually. The effect is more of small banks of pink clouds settling about the bush.

It may seem somehow fitting for so modest a rose, but I find it regrettable that knowledge of Betty Prior, the namesake, is apparently lost. What's known is that there was once a Prior firm, which bred roses and managed nurseries in Ipswich and Colchester, to the northeast of London. In 1935, after she had received a National Rose Society Gold Medal from the British Rose Society, 'Betty Prior' was introduced in the United Kingdom by Prior and, at about the same time, in the United States by Jackson and Perkins. No one seems to know whether Betty was a wife, daughter, niece, or granddaughter. Prior introduced other popular roses, including 'David Prior,' presumably named after a relative of Betty's and very popular until the 1960s, when it was lost. Sometime before that, in the 1950s, the Prior firm itself disappeared from the nursery world, and that is where their story ends.

I have owned two plants of 'Betty Prior.' One was already in place at our first home when my wife and I moved there, and I was quickly taken by its modest demeanor and nonstop flowering. That first plant stood at the back of a small bed that was tucked into a corner of the house. The site received decent, though not blazing, sunlight through the morning, but nothing direct or even very strong in the afternoon. What the location lacked in sunlight it made up for in moisture; in three seasons the rain from a downspout pooled at her feet, and in the fourth snow collected in the V between two adjacent roofs cascaded onto her. During the five years we lived in that house, I watched this dismal situation and vowed that I would right matters, but there was always some other planting to do, some other, more dire matter needing attention, and she stayed put. When we left, one day in late autumn, she was covered in blooms, and I imagine she still is.

When we moved to our present house and began to establish a garden, 'Betty Prior' was among the first dozen plants I ordered, and I gave her a key position in a stretch of mixed border. Behind her was an arborvitae hedge; on one side, a clump of zebra grass, *Miscanthus sinensis* 'Zebrinus,' and on the other, a creamy-yellow flowered broom, *Cytisus praecox* 'Moonlight.' The grass was an agreeable companion; its soft texture and fluid nature complemented the stiff, somewhat gangly character of 'Betty Prior' (and most roses, for that matter). The broom shared some of the same softening traits, and its great haze of yellow pea flowers contrasted handsomely with the early blooms of the rose. But one year we received a massive wet snowfall on April 1, and among the casualties was the broom, which was torn apart. So I dug it out, and left the area open until I could decide on a replacement (having at least decided not to have another broom). To fill the space, that summer I planted castor beans (*Ricinus communis*) at the back with *Browallia americana* in front of it. The browallia is a wandering thing, pulling itself up onto other plants where possible, and it found in the thorny canes of 'Betty Prior' a perfect ladder. By midsummer, the browallia had encircled the base of the rose; and its small blue flowers swung gaily from the lower branches.

It was a long and colorful alliance, during which I did little other than dead-head the rose and feed the browallia. They carried on together well into the fall, when the browallia finally collapsed from frost poisoning. 'Betty' soldiered on alone, scattering pink petals over orange maple leaves. The season concluded in early December with snow topping narrow buds waiting to unfurl. They were too late. Serious frost descended, and the remaining flowers withered and fell. The show came to a halt.

If you keep an eye out, you will see 'Betty Prior' carrying on in this fashion in all sorts of unlikely locations. There is, for example, a tiny garden filled with this rose at Sherman Square in New York City, an oasis the size of a small bedroom at the intersection of Amsterdam and Broadway near 71st Street. Should you happen not to make the sprint across the intersection and hold up on this midstream island, you will encounter a remarkable slice of greenery—a planting of 'Betty Prior' roses, nothing more—protected by wrought-iron fencing and thriving in the heat, wind, and drought of central Manhattan. The plants are as robust and healthy as any roses you will ever see, aided perhaps by the cleansing exhaust fumes that wash over the plants day and night, preventing mildew, black spot, and other fungal diseases. The display is a testament to 'Betty's' rugged constitution and a colorful reminder of nature's persistence and resilience in the urban jungle. I can't imagine a better plant for the job than the anonymous Ms. Prior.

Rosa 'Comtesse du Caïlla'

WAYNE WINTERROWD

'Comtesse du Caÿla'

⁂

R ECENTLY I PAID A VISIT to the Comtesse du Caÿla in New York.
Not the woman, who has been dead these hundreds of years, and
not the rose either, which was named in her honor in 1902 by the
great French rose nursery, the House of Guillot. It was the marble bust I visited,
carved by the sculptor Jean-Antoine Houdon in 1777. Since 1916 it has been at
the Frick Museum, where it is considered one of the treasures of the place.

It is a little thing, approximately twenty-six inches tall, on a carved base. But
it is made of fine white marble so skillfully wrought and so highly polished that
it seems larger than it is, and in certain lights its surface glows like living flesh.
Displayed are the head and shoulders of a lovely young woman in the first flower
of her beauty, barely twenty-two years old, with roses twined in her hair and
vine leaves draped about the garments that modestly conceal her breasts. She carries her head with dignity, her nose is straight and well formed, her forehead
broad, and her hair piled high, all qualities that bespeak nobility and moral seri-
ousness. But her cheeks are rounded, her chin is pointed, and her closed lips
barely suppress a flirtatious grin, details that suggest, with the roses and the vine

leaves, that she has been portrayed as a bacchante. Indeed, this bust, considered one of Houdon's masterpieces, has been much celebrated by critics for its juxtaposition of high nobility and youthful, frivolous joy, a juxtaposition that we do not see, obviously, in the famous statue of Houdon's friend and patron George Washington.

The lady in question, Elizabeth-Suzanne de Jauncourt (1755–1816), was indeed noble, becoming Comtesse du Caÿla upon marrying her cousin, François-Hercule-Philippe-Etienne de Baschi, Comte du Caÿla, in 1772, when she was seventeen years old. By what the Frick calls "creative etymology," the count's family declared itself to be descended from Bacchus, and that might in part explain Houdon's fanciful and charming realization. Or perhaps—great artist that he was—he simply perceived a contrast between a playful girl and her high place in the world, and chose to represent both aspects in one image.

But history has left us with two famous Comtesses du Caÿla, not counting the rose itself. The second was a commoner, born Zoë Tallon, and little is known of her until she was introduced into the court of the aged, obese, and gout-ridden Louis XVIII to amuse him in his final days. The King, born at Versailles in 1775, was the grandson of Louis XV and brother to both Louis XVI and Charles X, the latter succeeding him as the last of the Bourbon royal house to occupy the throne of France. Until he was nearly sixty, Louis was an embarrassment, a royal pensioner and a sort of kingly vagabond, spending a few years here, a few there, exiled from France and making his way from one court to another across Europe and even to England. But the fall of Napoleon in 1814 and the volatility of French politics brought him back to France as king that year, a position he occupied (with the brief interruption of Napoleon's return, the Hundred Days) for ten years. During this period, he seems genuinely to have done the best he could, even earning the praise of Queen Victoria. In his last four years, Zoë Tallon, made Comtesse du Caÿla, seems to have provided some comfort to a life that had become wearisome to him. Possessed of significant beauty as well as an agile mind and a fascination with politics, she quickly became a favorite of the old king, a position that allowed her to meddle in the confused affairs of France until his death in 1824, after which little is heard of her.

Unless, indeed, she is the woman Pierre Guillot wished to commemorate in 1902, when he created a new rose and named it 'Comtesse du Caÿla.' Somehow, one doubts that—indeed, hopes not. For the connection of so beautiful a rose with so beautiful a work of art as Houdon's bust would seem more fitting than its association with a courtesan who was active in a most unpleasant time in France's history, and who carried only a faint echo of the great French *maîtresses en titre*, such as Madame de Pompadour and Madame du Barry, into the time of Queen Victoria.

But however it is, when we consider this rose we are dealing with history, not only of two beautiful women of very different backgrounds and lives, but also of the venerable House of Guillot. Founded in 1829, it has continued through six generations to the present day, and now, under the direction of Jean-Pierre Guillot, markets over 250,000 plants a year while continuing to breed beautiful roses. Such a history is not in fact unique among French rose merchants, for the House of Meilland has also passed through six generations. Both houses have been responsible for remarkable achievements, Meilland most notably for the creation of 'Mme Antoine Meilland,' called 'Peace' throughout much of the world, and Guillot for 'La France,' the first hybrid tea rose, bred in 1867, and, in 1875, 'Ma Pâquerette,' the first *polyantha*. It is a curious thing, then, that 'Comtesse du Caÿla,' after a hundred years, should find itself featured on the Web site of the House of Guillot, with the comment that it is "still very much the fashion."

It could be that it is more the fashion than ever, for suddenly, worldwide, there is an interest in—almost a passion for—the progeny of *Rosa chinensis* 'Mutabilis,' of which 'Comtesse du Caÿla,' though its parentage is generally listed as unknown, is surely one. It is the signature peculiarity of *Rosa chinensis* 'Mutabilis' that its buds show coral orange when tightly furled, open to a clear silvery pink, and deepen to rose red as they mature. The blossoms are single, possessed of only five or so petals, and though frequently compared to butterflies, they often seem to be butterflies that have had a hard and windy flight. By contrast, the flowers of 'Comtesse du Caÿla' are technically doubled, and a single blossom might contain as many as eighteen petals arranged in a loose, luxuriant fashion, the center ones folded across a boss of clear yellow stamens. The color of these blossoms is often described as a blend of pink and salmon orange, but in fact an infinite gradation of those shades might be seen on a single bush, depending on the age of the individual flowers. And those flowers nod, as so many of the old French hybrids do, for the multiplication of their petals seems not to have taken account of the slenderness of their necks, or of the modern cut-flower market, which demands a rod-straight stem almost as thick as a wooden cooking spoon. No problem there, for they are very fine in the right sort of vase, or in the garden, when one lifts them gently up to view, as one would the face of a pretty child.

Technically, 'Comtesse du Caÿla' is often listed in references as a tea rose, which might be confusing to those gardeners who imagine that class best represented by 'Peace,' 'Mister Lincoln,' or 'Christian Dior.' For those are all vigorous plants, with big, opulent blooms on sturdy stems, the darlings of both the florist trade and the old lady next door. But they are modern hybrid teas, of course, a quite different thing from the original teas, which resulted from crosses of China roses with the Bourbon rose and with noisettes. To avoid this confusion, 'Comtesse du Caÿla' should properly be placed among the Chinas, as many authorities do, for not only its flowers but also its growing habit betray the heritage of that group. It forms a low, slight bush seldom taller than four feet, rather sparsely clad in leaves that begin—as do those of *Rosa chinensis* 'Mutabilis'—by being burgundy-colored and change as they mature to a dark olive green. Though the flowers smell of tea, which confuses matters a bit, they also carry the gentle but delicious fragrance of sweet peas. 'Comtesse du Caÿla' is in fact considered the most fragrant of the China roses, a class that has not generally inherited much of that desirable characteristic.

In the genus *Rosa*, with its approximately one hundred species and tens of thousands of cultivars, there are roses that will survive in almost any climate where gardening itself can occur, from USDA Zone 3, with brutal, thirty-below zero winter lows, to Zone 10, where even a light frost is a rare and devastating occurrence. In the case of 'Comtesse du Caÿla'—and, indeed, all roses that have inherited a large dollop of China-rose blood—temperatures of 10 degrees above zero Fahrenheit will begin to cause damage to twigs and stems, and an approach to zero degrees spells death. 'Comtesse du Caÿla' is therefore a tender rose—

always sad news for the preponderance of American gardeners, who garden in Zone 6 (winter lows of zero to minus 10) or colder. But, like all China roses, it does very well in a pot, provided one has the facilities to over-winter it, from October to March, in frost-free but quite cool conditions, such as a minimally heated garage, basement, or sunporch, or an unheated guest bedroom. There, it will weather out the temperatures that would kill it outdoors, come into growth in early spring, and bloom on a terrace or porch all summer long and well into autumn.

At my garden, North Hill, in southern Vermont, we maintain a cool greenhouse where tender plants are stored through the winter at temperatures of around 45 degrees. In it, among dormant fuchsias and agaves, winter-blooming species cyclamen, and a rare muscat grape called 'Datier de Leban,' are large pots of tender roses, all more or less tinctured with the blood of China. They include several specimens of *R. chinensis* 'Mutabilis,' the redoubtable 'Old Blush,' the deliciously yellow 'Lady Hillingdon,' the coral-pink 'Lafter,' and 'Comtesse du Caÿla,' which was brought here as a cutting from Christopher Lloyd's magnificent garden at Great Dixter, where it is one of the few roses he has chosen to retain from his mother's original collection. In the depths of winter, a routine visit to the cool, earth-scented lower greenhouse always lifts our spirits, for, by February, just as winter unleashes its last, desperate attack on us, the first leaves of the China roses will begin to unfurl, and soon the first coppery-pink buds will form. They are tiny then, stunted by dim winter light, a promise merely of what they will be in June. But as sleet-laden gales sweep over us, those buds offer something to hope for, and we know that, harsh as our climate can be, we will never give up gardening here, or growing roses. Among those roses, 'Comtesse du Caÿla' will always have a prominent place. Like any other rose, it lives a double life, being both itself, a mere flower, and also a suggestion of other people, places, and attitudes. So those first buds forming in the cold winter light remind us of the lovely girl at the Frick, or even of Zoë Tallon, whose warmth and beauty lightened the last years of the aged King Louis XVIII.

Rosa 'Bonica'

JULIE MOIR MESSERVY

Learning to Like Roses

I'LL ADMIT IT—I never really liked roses very much. Growing up in the fifties, I loved all the flowers of my mother's garden—lilies, bearded iris, snapdragons—but hated the hybrid teas. It was their vibrant colors and flamboyant names that repelled me: the vermilion 'Tropicana,' the velvet-red 'Chrysler Imperial,' the white-yellow-and-pink-petaled 'Garden Party.' They just didn't look right in our Illinois garden. Oh, yes, they smelled wonderful, each pungently different from the one next to it, standing tall and isolated from the other plants like exotic models on a runway. "Look at me—not her, but me!" they'd call, with thorns veiled but at the ready.

I've never enjoyed the amount of upkeep roses require either. We watched my mother struggle year after year with Japanese beetles and other pests and diseases—spraying, pruning, fertilizing. Later, after trying various products, like milky spore and neem-seed-oil spray, she finally garnered enough grandchildren to mobilize a crew of pickers. They'd all go down on summer mornings to the allée of old-fashioned roses for an hour of plucking and squeezing the beetles. Fun, if you didn't think about it too much. When the grandchildren grew too old for such directives, she finally gave up and eliminated all but the most resistant strains.

Alas, I've never much cared for rose gardens either. Free-thinking designer that I am, I dislike the obvious layouts, the symmetry and simplicity of the designs. To me, a rose garden is really just a display case for a series of prized specimens. Usually geometric, symmetrical, or axial in plan, the rose garden has one big idea: to show off its individual horticultural treasures—those high-strung models—to best effect. If you're someone who's not that interested in the plant itself, you'll find the typical rosegarden layout less than inspiring. One glance and you've seen it all.

Perhaps it's my own innate predilection for things that are imperfect, irregular, and modest that killed my interest in roses. For much of my life, I've been attracted to things Japanese, and roses don't figure much in the life of Japanese gardens. One finds them in American-style parks, yes—even circular rose gardens, or square ones with an arbor—but never have I seen a single rose in a traditional Japanese garden. Their absence probably has to do with the fact that the modern rose wasn't brought to Japan until the Meiji era, from 1868 until 1912, when intensive Westernization began there. Hybridized roses were introduced too late to become part of the indigenous culture that was dominated by the aesthetics of Zen and the tea ceremony. So, although they are *the* major cut flower for Western-style weddings and in Love Hotels, they are not a part of traditional culture.

Yet there are species of wild roses native to Japan that are lovely. Cuttings from these are used in flower arrangements, or artfully placed as single-stemmed specimens in a *tokonoma*—the alcove in the tea room where a scroll, a vase, and a simple spray of flowers are set out to celebrate the feeling of the day. In any case, flowers were rarely planted in traditional Japanese gardens except for iris and the blooms produced on woody shrubs such as azaleas, enkianthus, and andromeda. Even these would be pruned so that sparse flowering occurred. Prized peonies and chrysanthemums were often set out as specimen plants in containers on display, but were seldom actually planted in the ground.

Personality theory suggests that at midlife a subtle but significant change begins to take place in an individual's temperament. We begin to experiment with the sides of ourselves that we never favored before. Extroverts become more introverted; intuitives who have long lived in a world of imagination find themselves intrigued by the everyday sensory world; feelers become more interested in the rational; and spontaneous types become more structured and organized in their mode of operation. And so, at fifty-one, having been an extroverted, spontaneous intuitive all my life, I suddenly find myself interested in roses. I'm noticing their characteristics, coming to like their habits, and paying attention to their use in the landscape. I've even begun using them in my designs. I'm observing more carefully the way people grow roses, some of which delight me: the billows of *Rosa rugosa* just back of the dunes of ocean gardens; the climbers spilling over archways and up gutter pipes on English estates; the tall shrubby varieties that blossom from summer through late November, despite the frost's attempts to suppress them. I love the way some roses form soft hillocks that are surrounded by other flowers, coexisting modestly as members of a team that make up a garden's border. Indeed, it's the landscape roses that I love.

This sprawling class of roses includes 'Bonica,' the Meidilands, and the new hybrids from Canada: the Parkland and Explorer series. 'Bonica' is a medium-pink, double-flowering shrubby rose that grows three to five feet in height and four feet wide, possessed of a fruity fragrance, deep-orange hips, and dark-green glossy foliage. It and its sister, 'Royal Bonica,' offer attractive features when used in mass plantings or as a groundcover for poor soils. Developed by Meilland in France in 1982, 'Bonica' was the first shrub rose ever to be named an All-America Rose Selection (in 1987). 'Bonica' roses flower on their own rootstock, so if they die back during the winter they can recover in spring, growing vigorously from their roots.

The Meidilands are shrub roses also developed by the House of Meilland, and they are best used in public places and in smaller gardens as soft billows between perennials. Bred for disease resistance, glossy foliage, and heavy blooms, they are appealing for their vigorous, spreading growth habit, and can be used as a single specimen or wonderfully as a dramatic mass planting. The largest flower is the 'White Meidiland,' with as many as forty petals each; the 'Scarlet Meidiland' is a red semi-double plant with small cherry-pink blossoms and red hips in the fall. Both can cover whole hillsides as a tall ground cover, spreading by means of vigorous, self-rooting canes wherever they touch ground.

Canadian rose-breeders, hard at work to improve the winter hardiness of the landscape roses, have succeeded brilliantly with the new Parkland and Explorer series. Early attempts at growing roses in the Canadian prairie were often unsuccessful, because of extreme winter cold, and droughts and heat in summer. The Morden Research Station, part of Agriculture and Agri-Food Canada's research branch, was established in 1915, one of its charges being to develop hardy landscape plants. Starting with their first release, in 1929, researchers there have introduced more than 130 new hybrids to the nursery trade, including nineteen new cultivars of roses. The station's early roses, called the Prairie series, came from two parents, *R. pimpinellifolia* and *R. rugosa*, both hardy to minus 40 degrees Centigrade. The Parkland and the Explorer series later improved upon these early hybrids, with marked advances in flower quality, plant stature, and disease resistance. Early Explorer roses focused on hardy *rugosa* hybrids, resulting in 'Martin Frobisher' (1968), 'Henry Hudson' (1976), and 'David Thompson' (1979), to name a few, all honoring the men who first explored and mapped the nation that is now Canada. A breakthrough in the Explorer series occurred when *Rosa kordesii* was crossed with earlier hybrids, bringing more desirable characteristics such as smaller stature, glossy foliage, and improved flower quality. These newer varieties include 'Champlain' (1982), 'John Davis' (1986), and 'Frontenac' (1992). Two climbing roses were also developed, 'Louis Jolliet' (1990), and the superb 'Henry Kelsey' (1984), which has medium-red twenty-five-petaled flowers and spicy fragrance.

At the Morden Research Station, among the most popular are 'Morden's Blush,' a white rose developed in 1988 that flowers continuously into the fall, and 'Morden Centennial,' a two-to-three-foot lightly scented repeat bloomer with medium-pink flowers, introduced in 1980. I used it and the early Explorer series 'David Thompson' in the Toronto Music Garden, a project that I was fortunate enough to undertake with the eminent cellist Yo-Yo Ma.

A three-acre city park, the Toronto Music Garden answers this question: can a piece of music inspire the design of a garden? I must believe that the answer is yes. For, based on the First Suite for Unaccompanied Cello by J. S. Bach, this exuberant landscape is designed as a series of linked "movements"—in this case, garden rooms. The Prelude, Allemande, Courante, Sarabande, Menuett, and Gigue each suggest different natural imagery. The Prelude feels like a rocky riverscape, the Courante is designed as an exuberant wildflower hill with a maze-like path to its summit, the Allemande as a birch grove overtopping squirrel-trails, and the Sarabande is an inward-spiraling conifer dell. In the Menuett—the formal performance space perched high on a hill overlooking the harbor—I used fifty of the scented pink 'Morden Centennial' roses as a handsome backdrop to a perennial border that softens the base of native crabapple trees arrayed in a semicircle around a cobble-edged circular lawn. Movable benches are placed on the grass, facing a wonderful wrought-iron pavilion structure designed by local artist Tom Tollefson. Another fifty of the deep-pink-to-red-hued 'David Thompson' Explorer roses surround two weeping birches that bow and curtsey to each other while acting as a gateway into the last movement of the garden, the Gigue. This hillock of grass steps edged with the yellow-flowering coreopsis 'Moonbeam' is in the shape of a lyre and faces down into a weeping-willow tree that overtops a stone terrace "stage" for informal performances. Best of all, you can hear Mr. Ma play the suite as you walk through the garden, by renting an audio guide at the information center on the adjacent pier. The effect is magical.

So it is that, in the beginning of my dotage, roses are beginning to delight me at last. I'm learning that I can properly appreciate the many landscape roses by using them fluently in my new designs, and by trying out fresh combinations and creating innovative gardens that highlight overall composition as much as the individual specimen. With the disease resistance and cold-hardiness of the newer landscape roses, I don't need to worry as much about maintenance as my mother did. But who knows—as I grow older, maybe I'll need a bigger challenge, after all. Pretty soon, you may find me in my rose garden, pinching the Japanese beetles off my 'Tropicanas' and 'Chrysler Imperials.'

Rosa 'New Dawn'

JANE GARMEY

'New Dawn'

EVEN AS A CHILD, I knew roses were tricky. I learned that much from an aunt who was a passionate rosarian—a term that, because I was educated at an English convent school, conjures up an aged nun telling her rosary beads at all hours of the day. That was not my aunt. But when it came to the care and well-being of her roses, nothing was too much trouble. Having read somewhere that an Englishwoman living in Kenya claimed fresh elephant dung had miraculous effects on the vigor and growth of her roses, she was determined that her own roses should have the same treatment. Finding a supply of elephant dung in the south of England was not easy, but this did not deter her. She drove to Whipsnade Zoo, almost sixty miles away, made friends with the elephant keeper, and worked out an arrangement whereby she could take away as much dung as she wanted as long as she provided the containers and did the shoveling.

And so it was that trips to the zoo, first with her children, later with her grandchildren, became regular events on her summer calendar. As a child, I was envious of my cousins' good luck. My parents' interest in animals was limited to racehorses and Yorkshire terriers. Years later, however, I learned that my cousins had in fact loathed those expeditions, when each one was issued a bucket and spade and told to dig. Worst of all, they told me, was the long ride home, crowded into a hot station wagon redolent of fresh elephant dung.

Many years later, as a novice weekend gardener, I tried growing roses myself. Alas, lacking any elephant dung (there being no zoo to speak of in northwestern Connecticut), my roses drooped and pined. "Treat them as annuals, it's less depressing," suggested a helpful friend, herself an experienced gardener. This wasn't such bad advice. For two or three years I struggled to coax a few seductively named prima donnas into bloom, but they were a fairly intransigent lot and seemed to contract every possible ailment. There was, however, one exception—an adorable, good-natured climbing rose that I had picked up at my local nursery. Wanting a climbing rose, I had been trying to make up my mind between 'Pierre de Ronsard' and 'Clair Matin' when the nursery owner took one look at me and asked if I had considered 'New Dawn.' Well, to be perfectly honest, I had been put off by the name, which reminded me of dish detergent or shampoo, and had eliminated it from my list of possibilities. "Forget the name," he told me. "It's pretty, it's foolproof, and it will work . . . even for you."

He was, of course, right. Within a year, 'New Dawn' was bounding up, over, and around a trellis, sending out a profusion of the prettiest, palest-pink buds, reblooming in September, and demanding almost nothing by way of special care or attention. All the while, my other roses continued to languish.

About this time, Christopher Lloyd publicly declared that he was finished with roses, ready to throw in his trowel and banish them from his extraordinary garden at Great Dixter. In the garden world, this piece of news was greeted with the consternation that attended Martin Luther's nailing his ninety-five theses to the door of that church in Wittenberg. Rose growers all over the world were shocked and horrified. Not me. I was delighted. If those pesky creatures were to be exiled from the garden of the great Christopher Lloyd, why on earth could not I follow suit? Whither the master trod, I would follow. Out with them! And out they came. With one exception, of course—'New Dawn.'

These days, I waste no time looking through rose catalogues. Not for me the seductive charms of 'La Reine Victoria' or 'Mme Isaac Pereire.' I'm done with these fragile antique beauties, these martyrs to black spot, rust, and mildew. The only rose I put up with is common, ordinary 'New Dawn.' "Best-selling rose we have," says many a nursery owner I've talked to.

My pedestrian favorite, I have discovered, occurred in 1930 as a "sport." This is the technical name for a spontaneous bud mutation that gives rise to a new cultivar. It was the discovery of one Dr. Van Fleet, a distinguished American rose-breeder about whom curiously little is known. Why, I wonder, did he give it such a unprepossessing name? But it seems churlish to complain about a mere name when 'New Dawn' behaves so well in all respects. After all, didn't someone once say, "A rose by any other name would smell as sweet"? True, this is a rose that could not be described as sumptuous or dazzling. "Slightly tubby," is how the well-known rosarian Peter Beales describes its buds. However, both he and that other noted authority, Graham Stuart Thomas, are not stinting in their praise. For them, 'New Dawn' is: "deliciously fragrant," "the ideal smaller rambling rose."

This summer I visited Powis Castle and its extraordinary garden, built on many levels and buttressed by massive yew hedges. At one point, one passes through an opening onto a huge lawn bordered by a gravel path. On either side are roses growing up the remains of tree trunks, arranged in matching pairs. A nice idea, but not, when I visited, a successful display. Perhaps elephant dung was in no greater supply in that part of Wales than in my part of Connecticut. For, though it was still midsummer, all the roses supposed to be furled and looped around their posts in voluptuous bloom—'Kathleen Harrop,' 'Phyllis Bide,' 'Alister Stella Gray'—were taking a rest, to put it charitably. Except, that is, for one. It looked familiar. Could it be? Yes, of course it was. There, in far-off Wales, in full bloom, in this very famous garden, was my tubby little vulgarian, with an elegant marker distinctly identifying its name—'New Dawn.'

Rosa chinensis 'Bengal Crimson'

ROSIE ATKINS

Rosa chinensis *'Bengal Crimson'*

‿

T O BE HONEST, roses are not a particular passion of mine. When you discover a rose covered in blooms almost all year round, however, you cannot fail to be impressed. But, then, 'Bengal Crimson' is an extraordinary rose flourishing in an extraordinary garden. Let me tell you more.

The Chelsea Physic Garden was founded by the Worshipful Society of Apothecaries in 1673. In that year, they acquired a lease on some farmland that had access to the River Thames because they needed a boathouse for their gaily painted barge, which was used by the Apothecaries in pageants as well as for their herborizing expeditions. They built two other boathouses that were sublet to the vintners and the tallow-chandlers. In those early days, the Apothecaries grew plants to produce medicines, and apprentices collected plants and brought them back to the garden for study and proper identification. Thus, the Chelsea Physic Garden was soon established as a garden dedicated to the study of useful plants, a key step in the development of the branch of science we now call ethnobotany.

Today, the river is divorced from the garden by a feat of Victorian engineering called the Embankment, and the boathouse has become private property used for parking, storage, and beekeeping. But the proximity of the river, the garden's south-facing slope, its freely draining soil, and its high brick surrounding walls provide the place with a unique microclimate. It is said to be two degrees warmer than the Royal Botanic Garden at Kew, a few miles upriver, and tender plants thrive with a minimum of protection. The largest olive tree growing in Britain provides the Chelsea pigeons with a feast each year. The banana and tree ferns are huge, and a shiny-leafed grapefruit tree yields enough fruit to make marmalade.

More than ten years ago, I worked at the Chelsea Physic Garden as a volunteer gardener while I balanced a career as a journalist with being a mother of two. I saw the garden as a wonderfully therapeutic place, an escape from the computer, a way of getting my hands dirty and learning something new. Being given various horticultural tasks by the head gardener was far better for me than going to any gym or relaxation class. So, when, in November 2001, I was offered the post of curator, with its historic house and constant access to the garden, it was like being given the keys to Paradise.

What stopped me in my tracks on that misty morning as I walked up through the garden from the boathouse was not the olive tree or the banana, but a bush of burnished foliage beside the Swan Walk gate, covered with a mass of single magenta flowers. The label read *Rosa chinensis* 'Bengal Crimson.' I was still reeling from the previous night's Yeomanry Dinner with the Worshipful Society of Apothecaries, an experience heightened by the fact that I was still standing after a six-hour farewell lunch with my colleagues from *Gardens Illustrated*, the magazine I had launched and edited for ten years. At the end of the Apothecaries dinner, a bowl of rose water had been passed around, and I was instructed to dip my linen napkin into the scented water and dab it behind my ears, where it stimulates a nerve that encourages digestion. (This was not a practical joke, I promise you. Roses have been valued as medicinal plants for centuries. Our native dog rose, *Rosa canina*, has been used in infusions to treat tired eyes, and has also been made into a diuretic to treat kidney and bladder stones. Rose-hip syrups and jams have long been known as a potent source of vitamin C.)

On encountering *Rosa chinensis* 'Bengal Crimson' in the Chelsea Physic Garden, I was stunned by its beauty and wondered how it came to be there. I discovered that its history coincided with that of Chelsea Physic in several important ways. Its label recorded that the rose was introduced into cultivation in 1887, six years after the Worshipful Company of Apothecaries ceased to be responsible for the management of the garden, though they have continued in close association to the present day. A plant had been donated to the garden under the name 'Rose de Bengal' by the garden of the Royal Horticultural Society at Wisley in 1983, the date at which Chelsea Physic Garden became a charitable trust and first opened its gates to the public.

Many rosarians have tried to check the identity of the rose that graces the Swan Walk gate at Chelsea Physic Garden. Records show that it was initially determined to be *R. chinensis* 'Miss Lowe,' but a taxonomist working at the garden identified it as *R. chinensis* 'Crimson Bengal' on the basis of information about its typical size and the color of its blooms supplied by Peter Barnes at Wisley. So the name *Rosa chinensis* 'Crimson Bengal' went on the label when the present plant was planted in 1986 by Duncan Donald, then Curator of the Garden.

After ten years editing a garden magazine, I know the importance of correct plant identification, and how fraught with anxiety the process can be. I well remember how the burden on our editorial shoulders was lightened when Dr. James Compton, then head gardener at Chelsea Physic Garden under Duncan Donald, agreed to come into the offices of *Gardens Illustrated* to check that plant names matched the pictures and made sense in the text of every issue. However, the welter of epithets surrounding 'Crimson Bengal,' including *Rosa indica*, *R. sinica*, and *R. nankiniensis*, might have worried even Dr. Compton. Varietally, it has been called 'Miss Lowe,' 'Miss Lowe's Variety,' '*Sanguinea*,' and of course 'Bengal Crimson' and 'Crimson Bengal,' associating it with a number of other roses that are called "Bengal" simply because they initially reached Europe via India. In the midst of this nomenclatural muddle, I consulted Peter Beales, a great authority on roses in England and the proprietor of a great rose nursery. At his nursery, Simon White told me that our rose at Chelsea could safely be considered 'Bengal Crimson' but was, like its close relative *Rosa chinensis* 'Mutabilis,' quite tender (hardy barely to 10 degrees Fahrenheit) and, unlike that famous rose, was not particularly easy to propagate. Peter Beales's nursery had only six plants available when I placed my call.

I am obviously not alone in being excited about this rose, which is grown around the Garden rather like a signature plant. The Garden closes its gates to the general public at the end of October, but it remains open throughout the year to Friends of the Garden. One such visitor contacted me recently, leaving a distraught message in my voice-mail box. She was a garden designer who had just finished designing a garden for a client, and they had both come to visit the Chelsea Physic Garden to celebrate.

"We visited the Garden in November and saw *Rosa chinensis* 'Crimson Bengal' in full flower. We have looked in the *Plant Finder* and it is not there!" went her message. Her voice reached a crescendo of desperation as she concluded, "Please call me and tell me how we can get this rose. We would be prepared to pay to be allowed to take cuttings. It is simply the most beautiful rose I have ever seen. I have to have it!"

Why is this rose, with its magnetic appeal, so elusive and so little seen in commerce or in gardens? After all, it is blessed with wonderful foliage, and (at least in favored climates) with flowers throughout the year. Also, its history—an important thing in a rose—goes back to the Orient. Does its obscurity hang merely on the uncertainty of its name?

This possibility has caused me to ponder anew the importance of keeping records and continuing to verify plant identifications in my position at Chelsea Physic Garden. It is, after all, part of the inheritance I assumed when I became curator. For, since Linnaeus visited the garden in the eighteenth century, we often have found ourselves in the center of taxonomic debates. I hope the garden, in the spirit in which it was originally founded in 1673, will continue to excite students of botany as well as the general public and help them to understand the importance of correctly naming plants.

Were we able to propagate 'Bengal Crimson' at the Chelsea Physic Garden, I am sure we would have no problem selling plants, despite its tender nature. But we are a botanic garden, not a nursery. So those who wish to locate this extraordinary plant, full of both beauty and history, should perhaps get in touch with Mr. Peter Beales, straightaway.

Rosa filipes 'Kiftsgate'

CYNTHIA WOODYARD

'Kiftsgate'

⌒

MY ROSA FILIPES 'KIFTSGATE' STORY begins several years ago, maybe twenty, in a sweet and innocent enough, garden-friendly way, with my friend Susan bearing a gift, a potted rose. It was a big ugly thing—rough, brown, thorny, chopped—which my friend thought was called something like 'Night's Musk.' She described it as a fragrant white climber that grew quickly. Apparently her husband, who had been studying and collecting roses for some time, realized an error in his ways when this rose consumed one small tree and was headed toward a larger one. So he had decided to give it away. Who could resist a rose called 'Night's Musk,' suggesting all kinds of intriguing images and aromas? I was delighted with the gift, especially as I had what I thought was the perfect empty spot for it. Into a bed it went at the back of my garage, where I imagined it artfully pruned into a beautiful, fragrant wall-covering. It would greatly enhance the herb garden and the terrace nearby, and it could be viewed and even sniffed from the windows of the house.

For a couple of years, it grew just as I had imagined, nicely obeying my wirings and prunings. And when it bloomed, it perfumed the air with the most perfect English shed-garden-house-barn-without-cows fragrance, one I knew well from having spent so much time in England, lurking around gardens as a professional garden photographer. But as time passed, the rose began reaching beyond my original intentions. I like to think of myself as one who gratefully accepts the gifts of nature, and so I allowed the questing rose the freedom to join a fragrant, yellow-flowered honeysuckle that already draped along the gutter line. It was a good association, and the rose continued to look quite effectively trained. All went well for two or three years more, until the rose began breaking free even of its enlarged space, shooting out over the bed and into the walk, snatching hats and glasses and ripping holes in silk shirts with its large, hooked thorns. These repeated attacks on me and on visitors caused me to come to terms with the fact that this rose was not going to be the perfect, semi-espaliered rose of my dreams. Obviously it would have to be allowed more freedom, especially as it was bent on taking it anyway. Thinking I was still in charge, I let it climb up the garage roof for several more years of pain and bloodletting. I tried my best to keep it there, and to maintain some order by pruning madly and tying in the rebellious canes. All the while, as it was wildly swinging its ever-lengthening, wicked arms, it was producing more flowers, perfuming the whole garden for a week or two of pure bliss in June, and then producing hundreds of scarlet hips in autumn. But nobody was willing to help me prune it at that point, and so I decided simply to let it go the way it wanted. I softened, I gave in, I gave up, exactly as one does when one has completely fallen in love.

A seventy-year-old shore pine partially hangs over the garage roof, not a pretty tree by any means, with its sparse and spindly lower branches. The obvious solution for the rose was to let it climb into the tree. Once I turned loose of my illusion of control, the rest was easy. The rose required no help from me. Its grasp was firm and its desire was great. So up it skyrocketed. Its newly granted freedom caused it to grow a thorny structure that connected the old garage to the old pine, actually creating a stabilizing effect for both of them during high winds and even earthquakes. The bloody wrestling match between me and the rose was finally over. And, actually, neither it nor I could have been happier, for it was free at last, and I had a splendid show, high above my head.

Now, by March or April, the scrawny old pine is beautifully clothed in rose leaves that emerge wine-red and turn to a healthy, glossy green as they mature. Each leaf is composed of five to seven individual leaflets, and hangs on a delicate stem that bobs in the breezes. (*Filipes* does mean "threadlike" or "with threadlike stems," allowing graceful movement.) June brings an avalanche of creamy buds that open to single, cupped, inch-wide white flowers centered with a prominent boss of golden stamens. Flowers are borne in thick, dome-shaped panicles, or clusters, and Mrs. D. H. Binney, the owner of the original 'Kiftsgate,' once counted 428 individual blossoms in a single panicle. The rich yellow stamens tremble and buzz with bees, and the constant dusting of white petals fallen on heads, the walk, and the flower beds below simply adds to and prolongs the moment of beauty, in a romantic-wedding sort of way. In autumn, the leaves take on russet and rose and gold—all the colors of a ripe pear—before they fall, leaving behind thousands of shiny little red hips that persist long into the winter, feeding birds and dropping to the ground to germinate. (Gifts for friends!) Everything about this rose affirms the power of Nature, at least when assisted by the humility of the gardener, who must sometimes simply throw in the towel.

I am not the only one to appreciate this rose. In the sixty-four years since Mrs. J. B. Muir, the original creator of the famous gardens at Kiftsgate Court (Campden, Gloucestershire) planted it, it has attracted many admirers. Vita Sackville-West in her *Gardening Book*, for example, lyrically describes the effect of this rambler beautifully draped in an old apple tree, "with pale-green, dangling trails and clusters of yellow-centered flower . . . with myriads of the golden eyes looking down at you from among the lace." She felt the rose was best appreciated "on the perfect summer evening when everything else is breathless, and one just sits, and gazes, and tries to sum up what one is seeing, mixed with the sounds of a summer night—the young owls hissing in their nest over the cowshed, the bray of a donkey . . ."

Romantic as that evocation may be, Miss Gertrude Jekyll, who prided herself always on practicality and sensibleness, sees another use for the rose. In *Gertrude Jekyll on Gardening*, she commended it for camouflaging or enhancing any unsightly garden feature, and suggested planting it on "sloping banks, broken ground, as in old gravel pits or other excavations, [and] for all sorts of odds and ends of unclassified places about the home ground." Russell Page concurs in *The Education of a Gardener*, where he suggests it be used "where a green cover is needed." One supposes he has in mind some of our newer housing projects . . .

Interestingly, however, the exact identity of 'Kiftsgate' remains a botanical mystery. The first plants of *Rosa filipes* were brought into Western gardens in 1908 by the great plant explorer E. H. Wilson. According to Graham Stuart Thomas, Mrs. Muir bought and planted her specimen around 1938, but whether it was a hybrid of *Rosa filipes*, or a sport or seedling with unusual vigor, is not known. The species originates in temperate western China, which makes it hardy only in Zones 6 to 9, where it is capable of growing twenty feet in a season. Its relative tenderness poses no problem in my Portland, Oregon, garden, but of course would for the many American gardeners who garden in Zones 5 or colder, especially as 'Kiftsgate' will insist on waving high in the air, and the thought of attempting to lay it down and cover it is frightening.

In the mid-eighties, just shortly after I had planted my own rose, I wrote to Mrs. Diany Binney, asking if I might visit her garden at Kiftsgate Court. She wrote back permission, and she could not have been more welcoming to the younger, hungry gardening sponge I was then. True to the character of the greatest English gardeners, she was full of interesting stories to share about people and things in the gardening world. Lawrence Johnston lived at Hidcote, just up the road, and had assisted her mother, Mrs. Muir, in laying out the original garden with strict color combinations in mind, an effect that A.G.L. Hellyer likened to "the colors . . . of fine old tapestry." Mrs. Binney inherited Kiftsgate Court in 1954, and, having her own ideas about plants, she took courage in hand and laid out borders with interesting foliage combinations against her distinguished mother's work. She opened new areas of the garden, and built a beautiful half-moon swimming pool over the edge of the cliff overlooking the valley below.

As I listened to her stories and gardening experiences, I found myself staring at the huge plants climbing the trees, and even the old stone house. At that point, I had no idea that my mystery rose, clambering already over my garage, was actually a descendant of the huge roses in Mrs. Binney's garden, the oldest of which, planted by her mother, now measures one hundred feet in width and fifty feet in height, and has essentially digested a copper-beech tree. It is considered the largest climbing rose in England. If I had understood then that my rose was *that* rose, I could have saved myself a long and thorny battle, by simply giving in from the start. For Mrs. Binney had quoted, in Rosemary Verey's *The English-woman's Garden*, a writer who had discussed the rose in the *RHS Journal*, saying that *Rosa filipes* 'Kiftsgate' "would seize its chance to overpower all around and cover the ramparts of a Sleeping Beauty palace." My garage is not a Sleeping Beauty palace (one could wish), but it certainly was on the edge of being over-powered, until my 'Kiftsgate' found its tree.

But, odd as it may seem, in hindsight I feel that my participation in the long battle with that rose was extremely satisfying—a relationship, in a way. I wonder if the pain and struggle couldn't be likened to giving birth and then forgetting the pain, especially when the offspring grows up to be so beautiful. And as my collection of well-illustrated rose books grew, and I searched in vain for the mysterious 'Night's Musk,' a veil finally fell from my eyes, or was lifted. For there it was, my rose, in a recognizable photo, with a perfectly accurate description, in Peter Beales's *Roses*.

Thank you, Susan, for such a splendid gift.

Rosa banksiae 'Lutea'

KEN DRUSE

Rosa banksiae *'Lutea'*

⁊

ONE FAVORITE EPISODE from the annals of my personal horticultural career concerned a visit to my Brooklyn backyard by dignitaries from local public gardens one day in May. The occasion was the blooming of the Lady Banks rose behind my 1873 brownstone. *Rosa banksiae* 'Lutea' was covered with clusters of double, one-inch, butter-colored flowers that dangled like cherries. Everyone had the same comment, but it was not about the profusion of bloom, or the shower of petals when the breezes blew. Instead, they chorused, "You can't grow that here!"

Despite the evidence, they continued to repeat their contention. "It's not hardy," declared one visitor. "We grow it in the greenhouse," said another. "The best ones I've seen are in northern California," said a noted traveler. "No," answered a fourth, "Charleston, South Carolina." Yet, right beside them, a ten-foot-tall, four-inch-thick trunk pushed up from the ground. The trunk was reddish brown and covered with long strips of shaggy bark. Smooth, thornless green canes pressed skyward above the ragged base. Two stainless-steel cables, four stories high, were laced with the coppery new shoots. Regardless of the onlookers' doubts, the rose was plainly alive and well and living in Brooklyn.

The original Lady Banks rose was named for Dorothea Hugessen (1758–1828). That plant grew from a seedling of the species *Rosa banksiae*, named for Hugessen's husband, Sir Joseph Banks (1743–1820), one of the greatest botanical explorers and plant promoters of all time. Banks was appointed honorary director of Kew in 1772 and, in 1778, president of the Royal Society of London, the most prestigious scientific organization of the time. He was knighted for his contributions to science in 1781, and remained president of the Society until his death.

Sir Joseph Banks loved plants as a boy and studied botany at Oxford. As a naturalist, he joined a voyage to Newfoundland and Labrador in 1767. Although he did not publish an account of this expedition, he established a collection and made it available for scientific study. That same year, Banks was elected a Fellow of the Royal Society. Through the Society, he was able to join James Cook on the legendary voyage aboard the *Endeavour* (1768–71), which sailed into Botany Bay in April 1770. Linnaeus, the inventor of the binomial system of assigning plants and animals a two-word name (genus and species), was so impressed by the quantity of new species Banks recorded that he proposed the discovered land be called Banksia. However, it is called Australia, and *Banksia* became instead the name of a genus of thirty species of tender shrubs from that continent.

Although he could not later return with Cook to the settlement they had established in New South Wales, Banks became influential in its government, and in Pacific exploration in general. It was Banks who sent Captain William Bligh to collect breadfruit on the ship called the *Bounty*, now best known for the mutiny of April 1789. But despite this ill-fated voyage, Banks was successful in sending botanists to all parts of the world, often funding expeditions with his own money. His collectors sailed to the Cape of Good Hope, West Africa, the East Indies, South America, India, and China. Of the many plants honoring Banks, the Lady Banks rose—discovered in China—is probably the best-known in the United States.

Roses were popular in the Old World, of course, from ancient times, and many varieties of the European species were widely grown. But the introduction of the first Chinese roses in the mid-eighteenth century caused a sensation. These tender roses rebloomed, and had the fragrance of tea. A rose procured by Banks in 1789 proved hardier than the earlier ones, and by the 1820s, the 'Common Blush,' 'Old Blush,' or China rose, as it variously was called, grew in gardens all over England.

The China and tea roses were not the only ones discovered in the Orient and brought to England. Four forms—single and double, yellow and white—of what was to be called *Rosa banksiae* arrived in England. This handful of roses, designated botanically as *R. banksiae*, was given its popular name by Robert Brown, the taxonomist for Banks's collections. Some of the cultivars have thorns, and most are fragrant. The double yellow Lady Banks is both thornless and scentless. But what the blossoms lack in perfume they more than make up in sheer numbers. The year of the visit by professional gardeners to see my plant in Brooklyn, I mapped out a square yard and counted the blossoms therein. I divided that sum into the footage the plant occupied and came up with an astounding number. My Lady Banks carried approximately ten thousand flowers.

Temperatures below zero degrees Fahrenheit can be expected in the Brooklyn garden, and that would classify this place as being in USDA Zone 6. However, in the last decade, the temperature has only touched zero degrees twice, and not gone below. Some temperature-zone maps show Brooklyn as being part of Zone 7, and I suppose 7b would most accurately describe this last, unusually warm decade. Most books list the hardiness of the Lady Banks rose to be in USDA Zones 8, 9, and 10, where minimum temperatures range from 10 to 40 degrees Fahrenheit. To be fair, the Brooklyn garden has what could be considered a perfect description of a microclimate, Brooklyn being on Long Island, which is surrounded by water. Large bodies of water do not change temperature as quickly as air, so the climate is moderated. The pavement and the brick and stone buildings absorb and radiate heat. My rose is on an east-facing wall, and the house protects the garden from winter winds. There is enough sunlight for Lady Banks to perform well, but not enough to cause winter sunscald to the semi-evergreen leaves and the young canes, or to cause flower buds to warm and open too early and be nipped by late frosts. The soil may be warmed by the building's foundation, but, more important, in summer the earth is cool and moist for the roots.

Whatever allows the Lady Banks rose to thrive in my garden, the horticulturists who visited that day were confounded. Whether it was the vigor of this plant from a genus known to need coddling, or reference books that printed and reprinted the notion that the species would die at 10 degrees Fahrenheit, the witnesses seemed to need more than their eyes to shake their preconceived beliefs.

In 1937, Robert Ripley, of "Believe It or Not" fame, traveled to Tombstone, Arizona, the Town Too Tough to Die. Unlike the gunfighters who had passed through that place in the bad old days, a Lady Banks rose, planted in 1885, had stayed on. It had grown into what was rumored to be the world's largest rose, and Ripley was on his way to see it. The rose had been planted by Mary Gee, the Scottish bride of a mining engineer, who pined for her verdant homeland. To help, her family sent cuttings of shrubs from home, including a Lady Banks rose, which she planted in the backyard of Cochise House, now called Rose Tree Inn. The rose was trained to grow as if it were a tree, its spreading branches supported by iron pipes. Today, it covers eight thousand square feet, with a trunk that has a twelve-foot circumference.

The rose in Tombstone, Arizona, made it into Mr. Ripley's newspaper column as the largest one in existence, a record it still holds. I am not sure if my guests, encountering so huge a rose growing in the desert, would have believed that, or not.

Rosa chinensis 'Old Blush'

THOMAS CHRISTOPHER

Rosa chinensis *'Old Blush'*

P ROUST may have had his madeleines, but I have the China rose 'Old Blush.' What's more, I got the better part of the deal. Hiding in a cork-lined room to wallow in carbohydrates may have satisfied the Parisian novelist; to me, though, it seems a recipe for boredom and obesity. I'd much rather be out driving the back roads, prowling the countryside, and burgling graveyards. That's where 'Old Blush' has taken me. It still does, too, though recently only in Proustian recollection.

Mind you, this is not a rose that ever won awards and medals; 'Old Blush' never was and never will be named an All-America Rose Selection. It is handsome, if unspectacular, as a shrub—a dense, upright mound of medium-green foliage that can reach a height of five or six feet in the Deep South. That's where 'Old Blush' is most at home, though with irrigation it thrives also in the Southwest. It is sensitive to cold. In the past, I have repeated the assertion that 'Old Blush' is hardy to USDA Zone 5. Secretly, though, I suspect that this rose would be little more than root-hardy north of Zone 7. Yet it is true that I once found a flourishing, albeit small (three-foot) specimen in the garden of two elderly sisters in Kansas City, Missouri.

There was no mistaking the thing. The clustered blossoms, casual three-inch cups of clear pink petals, though lovely, lack the elegance of a modern hybrid tea, but they also have the virtue of persistence. 'Old Blush' blooms incessantly from late spring until cold shuts down the bush in fall or winter. (I've picked flowers from 'Old Blush' in December in Texas.) The rate of flowering does decline temporarily in the heat of the summer, when the individual blossoms seem to sunburn; in cooler weather, they blush (appropriately) to a deeper rose pink on the petal tips. Stick your nose in one of these flowers and you will discover, alas, that this rose is almost scentless. It is redolent of history, however.

Many of these memories are secondhand. Because I neither speak nor read Chinese, I have no access to the first experiences of this flower, apparently a fixture in Chinese gardens by the eighteenth century. I doubt it played a prominent role there, however, as the Chinese did not (and do not still) particularly esteem roses; their thorns are considered to make them inauspicious plants. I wish I could have been in Uppsala in 1752, though, when a Swedish ship's doctor presented a start of this plant to Linnaeus. What did that sex-obsessed naturalist make of this rose, with its fat, fecund hips?

Most likely, he regarded it as a curiosity, nothing more, for 'Old Blush' performs poorly in the pale, cool damp of Northern Europe. By 1789, it arrived in England, via the Netherlands, to which it had most likely been brought directly from China by some employee of the Dutch East India Company. Four years later, it surfaced as 'Parson's Pink China,' and attracted much attention from English gardeners simply because it bloomed repeatedly. The European roses of that time typically bloomed just once a year, in late spring or early summer.

Nurserymen and rose amateurs began to encourage a mating of the re-blooming pink with various European roses, and the potency of the Asian foreigner was such that it has been implicated in the birth of almost every class of modern rose. 'Old Blush' wasn't the only imported parent, but it was among the most important. English rosarians still refer to it (under the English name of Parson's, of course) with a mixture of awe and envy as one of the "four stud

Chinas"—a title only an Englishman could award or even repeat without tongue in cheek.

'Old Blush' figured in the breeding programs of American rose fanciers, too. But, at least in our sunnier climes, its success was also highly regional. This I learned during the four years I spent as a Yankee commuting to central Texas. Modern roses—hybrid teas and floribundas—were nothing but expensive annuals, I was told by the local gardeners. "Don't grow roses in the garden you are planting here," they warned. But then I was taken in hand by Pamela Puryear, native Texan and freelance savant. She educated while she entertained with stories about pioneer duels fought for the honor of a horse and other milestones of central-Texas history; she constantly quoted relatives who, it would emerge, had passed on decades or generations previously, and seemed able to put a Latin name on every local wildflower. Most important, Pam was (and is) a gardener, if more in spirit than in fact, and she loved the time-tested plants she found on old homesteads and in the lush, seemingly chaotic yards of elderly women of color.

Of course there was an order hidden in these gardens, and I gradually came to understand it. Trees were placed where the shade was most grateful, and shrubs were set where they could be watered by a pan of dishwater tossed out the door. Herbaceous plants were commonly allowed to choose their own location; though its forebears were originally imported as slips or seedlings, the generation that decorated a mature garden almost always sprang from volunteer seedlings, and it was the most vigorous seedlings, the ones that happened to have rooted in a propitious spot, that were spared the hoe.

These elderly women had no particular reverence for antiques, but they mostly grew heirloom flowers and shrubs because the premodern plants tended to be easier. The flowers might not be as spectacular as contemporary hybrids, but on the whole the old-time plants were self-reliant, well adapted to the local climate and soil, and they flourished with little care. Ease of propagation was also important, as the ladies planted only what they could have for free, passed along as slips or seeds from other gardeners. The poinsettia that a niece gave to them at Christmastime, the amaryllis discarded by a neighbor once the bloom had faded, these, too, went into the mix. The gardens were rich in glorious, often spectacularly tacky incongruities—a particularly choice specimen, the horticultural equivalent of a genuine Chippendale chair, was likely to be potted up in a rusted okra can.

Roses, grown from cuttings, were a common feature of these gardens, which turned out to be a unique repository of bypassed but hardy heirloom races and cultivars. 'Miss Mary Minor,' for example, a creamy pink discovered outside that lady's cottage in Anderson, Texas, turned out to be 'Souvenir de la Malmaison,' a French-bred Bourbon rose of 1843. Similarly, 'Martha Gonzales' from Navasota later emerged as 'Fabvier,' another French immigrant, a China rose introduced in 1832.

It was in the cemeteries, however, that I first met 'Old Blush.' Pam had an encyclopedic knowledge of country graveyards derived from her genealogical studies, and we hit all the high points. These were not the most scrupulously kept graveyards, but they offered something better than "perpetual care," the modern practice whereby planting by the bereaved is forbidden because it complicates the mowing; instead, the whole area was hoed up to keep it free of grass, and roses, the traditional flower for a mother's grave, were tolerated. Far better than either of these, however, were the neglected, half-forgotten burial grounds that received no attention other than an occasional cutting of the tall grass, where self-sown trees invaded the edges, and the roses flourished undisturbed. This described perfectly the Odd Fellows Cemetery in Anderson, which capped a low hill not far from Miss Mary Minor's house.

There were roses all over that burial ground. Most were petrified, stone blossoms carved into the lichen-smeared headstones. This is actually a pagan practice (though I doubt the good Baptists of Texas knew that). It harks back to burial customs of the Greeks and Romans, who dressed their dead in rose wreaths. To ensure a convenient supply of these necessary props, the ancients often planted rosebushes in their graveyards. So, too, someone long ago had planted a bush of 'Old Blush' in the Anderson graveyard.

When had this been done? Who can say? Pam told me of discovering a specimen of 'Old Blush' outside an abandoned cabin. Inside, she found newspapers that dated to the 1940s. Another self-taught historian of roses, Carl Cato of

Lynchburg, Virginia, later told me of a bush of 'Old Blush' that he had found outside the house in Appomattox where Lee surrendered to Grant; in the Mathew Brady photograph of that event, Carl had found a shrub that looked identical growing in the very same spot.

The significant fact about the 'Old Blush' I met with in the graveyard was that, despite years or even decades of neglect, it was in flawless health and enviable bloom. No one sprayed these roses, fertilized them, or even watered them in a region that might go months in summertime without rain. Standing in that cemetery and looking at that horticultural survivor changed my understanding of roses fundamentally and permanently. Roses, I know now, are not the difficult and demanding shrubs most gardeners think them to be, unless we insist on making them so.

My sojourn in Texas ended, and I returned to a Northern home where China roses do not thrive. I have an old pink damask captured in a Connecticut farmyard that is almost as rugged and carefree, a sort of Northern edition. It, too, is practically fungus-proof, and it flourishes without irrigation in its sunny spot along the driveway. It lacks the Southern rose's decorum, however; the unnamed damask has surrounded itself with suckers and clearly aspires to become a briar patch. And though the damask's flowers are sweetly perfumed, with the classic "old-rose" fragrance, they appear just once each summer, in a single flush, toward the end of June.

Above all, whatever its virtues, the Yankee rose doesn't carry the memories of 'Old Blush.' It is, in this respect, like the doughnuts we in New England eat with our coffee. Doughnuts are excellent things and you should be glad to have them. But they aren't madeleines.

Rosa glauca

JOE ECK AND WAYNE WINTERROWD

Rosa glauca *at North Hill*

W HEN A GARDEN GETS AS OLD AS OURS, its owners begin trying to remember how and when this or that plant came into it. As our garden was made from pure scratch, with two of us at work from the beginning, we tend to spend even more time musing over its history. It is a pleasant activity, akin to recalling old family stories, though to an outsider—especially a nongardener—it may sound a bit dotty. Maybe it is a bit dotty. But as we indulge in these memories mostly when we are alone—at rest in the garden with a glass of wine in the evening, or in the car on a long and tedious journey—we are not much exposed to the ridicule of others. Not that we'd care if we were.

The subject of these reminiscences can be almost any plant we think of, provided it has been in the garden for some time and its history is not fresh in our minds. Recently it was an old plant of *Rosa glauca*. We have only one, a rather gaunt old bush about six feet tall that stands in the left corner of the upper bed of the perennial garden, about midway between the stone wall that backs a line of antique apple trees and the three-foot stone retaining wall that holds that back bed above the lawn in the garden's center. Against that retaining wall there is—

has been for almost twenty years—an antique deacon's bench, now quite black from applications of linseed oil and the weather, where we sit a bit on fine evenings during most of the growing season.

The bench is long enough for two to sit comfortably and each rest a glass of wine, and it commands a view of the whole perennial garden, a rectangle about sixty feet long and forty feet wide, completely sequestered from the world outside by stone walls on three sides, a twenty-foot-high planting of arborvitaes against the road, and the four antique apple trees at its back. They also are grown now to twenty feet, with flaky, rough trunks as many inches around and limbs we can climb, though we remember planting all four when they were no thicker than a broomstick. 'Cox's Orange Pippin,' which lies most immediately behind the rose, is celebrated for its October ripening, its splendid orange color, and its taste, and is the best of all apples in our opinion. A yew hedge now over eight feet tall sequesters the perennial garden from the house beyond, and is dense enough to muffle even the insistent ring of the telephone.

In the center of this garden are three small panels of lawn, each about fifteen feet square, held up by stone retaining walls to form a series of broad planes, on the third of which the bench sits. Our garden is on a steep hill, so it is only by such contrivances that we can make level places. As the perennial garden is at one of the highest points, near the house, it commanded a fine view of the mountains on the far side of our valley—until we planted it out with pines and Serbian spruces, leaving only a tantalizing sliver. We forfeited that view, which really was very fine, for protection against the wind and a greater sense of enclosure for the whole garden, reasons we have never regretted. Higher in the air than the terracing and the pines, the bench on which we sit now receives the very last warmth of the sun that can be enjoyed in the garden. Only the vegetable garden lies higher, a stiff uphill walk through the pergola and then the upper meadow, where we will rise and go finally to feed the cows their evening bale of hay, close up the poultry, check on the pig, and gather greens for dinner.

On such a mellow evening last July, sitting on our bench after a long and satisfying day of tending the garden (which seemed to smile at us all day, as it can in July, when it is finally under our control), we noticed *Rosa glauca*. *Rosa glauca*

ECK
AND
WAYNE
WINTERROWD

200

originated in the mountains of Central Europe, endowed with a hardiness of at least Zone 4 (minus 30 degrees Fahrenheit). It travels through gardens still under the synonym *Rosa rubrifolia*, which persists because it is so nicely descriptive of the purple foliage. Because it is a species, seedlings true to their parent can be expected to occur. Graham Stuart Thomas, writing in *The Graham Stuart Thomas Rose Book*, captures, as always, the species' essential nature:

> There are very few shrubs with such distinctive garden value as this open-growing species, with no great pretensions apart from the colouring of its leaves. It is practically thornless, apart from the base of the strong violet-coloured young shoots . . . The growth and leaves resemble somewhat the Dog Brier, but all the leaves, from spring till autumn, have a unique glaucous colouring . . . The flowers are borne in bunches [and] are of a clear pink, enhanced by the white center area which in turn is crowned by light yellow stamens . . . Later the heps, of an unusual brownish-red, crop in bunches and give further colouring to the bush, as they are usually very free. Little scent.

With our *Rosa glauca* planted where we have it, the absence of scent matters little to us against its virtues, which are apparent from any distance. True, our one old bush, now occupying its place for at least twenty years, is rather sparse on its single thick trunk, and tall New England asters yet to flower press green against it. Still, it looked quite fine at that moment, with its small, purplish leaves glowing ("like stained glass," many authors have written) in the last of the sun. The leaves were enough to start us pondering. (Two voices, one memory. You may separate us if you can.)

"Where did we get that plant?"

"When did we even first know about it?"

"Surely it was from Marshall?"

Marshall Olbrich, with Lester Hawkins, was cofounder of the famous Western Hills Rare Plant Nursery in Occidental, California, and of a great garden there. The two were a crucial force in the creation of our own garden. We stumbled up their garden path, barely dry behind our ears, and they smiled on us with encouragement. Marshall remained a loyal and generous friend until his death in 1991. Lester had died in 1984, an early casualty of the disease we subsequently knew as AIDS. Marshall continued to visit here until his death, and to endow our garden with treasures, as does Maggie Wych, whose garden Western Hills now is, and whom we try to visit once a year at least.

"No. Marshall told us to write to Lily Shohan. She sent a list."

Lily Shohan, who still lives and gardens in Clinton Corners, New York—a place almost as cold as Readsboro, Vermont—was then secretary of the Antique Rose Society. We boldly wrote her twenty-five years ago to ask which old roses we could grow. She kindly sent back a two-page letter of warm encouragement, listing a dozen of the best. Among them were the meltingly pink 'Cuisse de Nymphe'; 'Mme Hardy,' with its crush of snow-white petals and its haunting green eye; the blood-scarlet 'Old Red Moss' (which Tony Lord, guiding light of the RHS *Plant Finder*, told us on a subsequent visit is really to be called by its French name, 'Henri Martin'); 'Tuscany Superb,' with June-born single flowers of a curious cinnabar red; and several *rugosa*s, most remarkably 'Hansa,' a tall, splendid rose with huge semi-double cerise flowers, the better-behaved 'Belle Poitevine,' of tender, bluish pink, and the incomparable *R. rugosa* 'Blanc Double de Coubert,' whose semi-double chalk-white flowers, we were to learn, were considered the best for fragrance by Vita Sackville-West, though Christopher Lloyd scorns them. Never mind. We love Christopher Lloyd to death, but they are here, and we think they are very fine.

Lily Shohan also recommended that we experiment a bit with roses not guaranteed to be completely hardy in our cold, Zone 4 garden. She especially commended 'Variegata di Bologna,' which is still with us from that early planting, having its good years and its bad, depending on how effectively its eight-foot canes are weighed down by protective snow. If there has been enough—or if we have remembered in autumn to spare a few evergreen boughs for the canes' protection—we will get five-inch blooms, cups of vanilla cream streaked and splotched with raspberry, smelling of nothing more than one dreams a rose should.

JOE
ECK
AND
WAYNE
WINTERROWD

202

"But after Lily's letter, where did we get all these roses? How did we know where to order?"

"It was Will Tillotson. Marshall told us to go to him."

Will Tillotson had been a good friend of Marshall Olbrich and Lester Hawkins, and, indeed, of all the brilliant nurserymen who clustered around San Francisco from the late fifties to the last years of the seventies. More than anyone in North America, he was responsible for what has been called the "Old Rose Revival," a movement that is still growing strong, stronger perhaps than ever. In her wonderful book *Onward and Upward in the Garden*, a collection of garden-catalogue reviews for *The New Yorker*, the late Katherine S. White had this to say about Will Tillotson:

> Another writer with a style of his own is Will Tillotson, the grower and catalogue writer for Will Tillotson's Roses, Watsonville, California. The two catalogues I have—1955 and 1956—were lent to me by a friend who runs a beauty parlor, and I must not keep them long, because though she has never bought a Tillotson rose, she reads Tillotson every night before she goes to sleep . . . Style and all, the Tillotson catalogues bring me great happiness . . .

By the time Lily Shohan wrote us, in the late seventies, Will Tillotson was dead, and his nursery had passed into the hands of his assistant, Dorothy C. Stemler, who rechristened it Roses of Yesterday and Today, and passed it on to her daughter, Patricia Stemler Wiley. From Mrs. Wiley we got all of the wonderful roses recommended by Ms. Shohan, though they were grafted onto stock of 'Dr Huey,' a squalid bruisy red-flowered rambler whose chief claim to fame is that it roots easily and withstands saline poisoning, a consideration where gardens are irrigated by water borrowed from the Colorado River. That is not a concern here in southern Vermont, though for many years we had to watch closely for shoots originating below ground on any of Mrs. Wiley's roses, for they would surely be 'Dr Huey,' vigorously reaching above ground, yet again.

JOE
ECK
AND
WAYNE
WINTERROWD

204

Our specimen of *Rosa glauca* was grafted (we remember that, at least), but we planted it a full six inches below graft union, as one should in cold climates, to encourage any grafted plant to form its own roots and make suckers, both for continuity and to spread about the garden. But our *Rosa glauca* has not made any suckers at all, whether of itself or of its graft parent. It stands alone, a fine craggy bush clad in pewtery-red leaves from early spring throughout the growing season, bearing rather ordinary single, five-petaled pink roses in June, and sprays of cranberry-orange hips in October, just as the apples on 'Cox's Orange Pippin' reach that same color. We cannot bear to cut it to ground, as we were once advised to do, in order to encourage fine, vigorous new shoots. We have, however, had a dialogue about this matter, in the early-summer twilight.

"Do you think we should chop it off?"

"Why?"

"Well, to produce vigorous new growth."

"I like it the way it is."

"So do I."

The pleasures of starting a new garden, fresh on the land, are very intense, and our single plant of *Rosa glauca* came to us when we would have said, with Miranda in *The Tempest*, "O brave new world, that hath such creatures in't!" A kind of Prospero—or, in this case, a Marshall Olbrich or Lily Shohan—might have answered, "'Tis new to thee."

The wonder, to us, is that it still is.

Logee's 'Rosette'

TOVAH MARTIN

Logee's 'Rosette'

⌒

UNCLE RICHARD PASSED AWAY last week, so I guess I'll have to tell you about Logee's Greenhouses and *Rosa* 'Rosette.' Uncle Richard was a greenhouse man, through and through. When he was younger, he bought a farm nearby. But the soil proved to be so poor that when the agricultural-extension experts came to advise him on crops there was much shaking of heads and talk of sheep, perhaps. So Uncle Richard was stuck in the greenhouse his father had established in 1892 in Danielson, Connecticut.

At night, he stoked the boiler, staving off the freezing cold for nearly an acre under glass, two stories tall. By day, he repaired broken panes or putzed around the potting benches. But mostly his daylight hours were spent perched in his chair by the desk in the greenhouse office, sound asleep but subliminally poised to wake as soon as a customer came through the front door. In his later years, he would inquire if they wanted a box in which to accumulate all the tropical plants he suspected they couldn't resist adopting. But earlier in his career, he would write up orders for bouquets or boutonnieres, or fetch his sister (my mother-in-law), Joy Logee Martin, to speak with a prospective bride.

Back then, they didn't fly flowers in from Holland. In fact, I can't recall a single instance when the Logee family bought cut flowers from any external source. And anyway, no one in the downtrodden little mill town could afford that brand of indulgence. So, during the winter, lots of stevia lined the aisles in lieu of baby's breath, and immense camellia trees—cultivated for corsages rather than propagation cuttings—monopolized one wall. But for all Uncle Richard's fiddling with valves and piping, the original, large greenhouse couldn't really be heated any warmer than 50 degrees Fahrenheit. So that's where the roses grew.

The *Rosa* 'Rosette' came into the fold in the 1950s, long before my time at Logee's. To hear Uncle Richard tell it, the rose was a reject from a University of Connecticut breeding program. What year its creation took place, and which professor was responsible, we'll never know, now that Uncle Richard is gone. But the mission of the breeding program was to produce roses of the sweetheart form, with one big, juicy blossom crowning each plump cane. Beauty incarnate in every other aspect, 'Rosette' turned out to be a floribunda, and so it persisted in branching into an expansive spray of half a dozen flowers. Needless to say, 'Rosette' was a failure from the perspective of the latest flower-market vogue, but the professor realized that his rose might find a niche with the crowd that favored hand-tied bunches. So it came to live in the big greenhouse, and in deference to its breeder, the Logees dubbed it "the Connecticut Rose," although no one ever called it by that nickname.

Deep, juicy, blood red, and blessed with a slow, dramatic unfurling process, a long shelf life, and a subtle fragrance that awoke the nostrils but didn't cloy, 'Rosette' hit its stride with a population dedicated more to economy than fashion. It fit the town—reliable and hardworking, but not overly ambitious. Most important, it was a bargain—lots of flowers at a modest price. It was a flower that a mill town could understand.

When I arrived, three huge bushes were interspersed with the tropicals, pruned and groomed to deliver armloads of blossoms, ministered to with all the respect afforded any cash cow. Joy had long since retired from the tribulations of wedding work, but Uncle Richard was still sending husbands down the steep steps to the greenhouses to see his sister, who (after trading a little gossip and comparing notes on the new clergy in town) brandished her pruners and snipped away, creating sumptuous anniversary bouquets, purchased as standing orders from year to year. The bouquet never varied. It was composed of only one protagonist—a dozen sprays of *Rosa* 'Rosette'—the same that had accompanied the blushing bride down the aisle. And for the twenty-five years that I was there, the price also remained as constant as the order—ten dollars a bouquet.

For his part, Uncle Richard cut roses only in an emergency, when his sister wasn't on hand and the customer couldn't be stalled. The problem wasn't lack of competence, but, rather, territory. *Rosa* 'Rosette' was Joy's domain, and on the few occasions when Uncle Richard invaded it with pruning shears, tempers flared by nightfall.

Joy wasn't big on greenery. She might gather a few fronds of asparagus fern on the way up to the office, but mostly she relied on the deep bronze of the rose's shiny leaves as filler: fortunately, *Rosa* 'Rosette' boasted tidy foliage. She would ceremoniously bring her bunch up to the office, remove extraneous lower leaves and the few thorns, and needle Uncle Richard until he finally found the gift cards buried in his desk. Then the whole thing (and the circumference of a dozen stems of *Rosa* 'Rosette' is an armload to be reckoned with) was wrapped up gingerly in green waxed paper and handed over to the customer's safekeeping.

I guess it's a tribute to *Rosa* 'Rosette' to say that, year after year, the bushes always brandished sufficient blossoms to keep the couples of our town joined in domestic bliss. A dedicated performer, the rose never betrayed the scarcity of light to which it had been subjected in winter, or the greenhouse's tendency to turn clammy when temperatures plummeted, despite Uncle Richard's fondest attentions to the furnace. The rose thrived on adversity, producing blossoms intermittently year round. I remember tearfully cutting a spray on Thanksgiving Day one year, when I came home to find my pet turkey stuffed in a broiling pan. It was the only token of protest I could think of, seeing as Joy occasionally used 'Rosette' in funeral pieces, if nothing else presented itself.

Of course, there was much anxiety about botrytis and the proper sequence of fertilizing. During autumn and winter, there were occasional bouts of fungus. Spent buds might become soggy gray globs in no time flat, threatening to spread their condition like a plague to the rest of the shrub. But those were minor infractions in the realm of rosedom, and chances were, if Joy had collected a bouquet of *Rosa* 'Rosette' for your wedding, she would wangle a replay for anniversaries in perpetuity. You could count on it.

Other roses also took advantage of the conditions of the huge greenhouse. Someone had planted a climbing 'Cécile Brünner' to thread its way through the upper story, adding a sprinkle of tissue-pink blossoms that didn't require much care. Like the 'Rosette,' 'Cécile Brünner' was planted directly in the ground, in deep New England soil, under the relative warmth and protection of the greenhouse. And because Grandfather Logee had grown it, we persisted in keeping pots of *Rosa* 'Maréchal Niel,' a classic yellow tea-noisette, circa 1864.

We kept a number of other roses more for sentimental reasons than anything else. One, the *Rosa* 'Rouletii,' a quaint mini-rose that can easily be contained in a five-inch pot for years, has followed me out of the greenhouse and into my private home. Uncle Richard liked nothing more than to tell a story, and he claimed that 'Rouletii' was first collected in a Swiss village in 1922, and from those humble beginnings became the parent of all miniature roses. Of course, he also told how, once, he'd caught every pane of glass—unbroken—as it flew from the greenhouses during a hurricane, but I had no reason to doubt his claims as far as 'Rouletii' was concerned. And the fact was, that little rose deserved to start a trend. Of the tiniest stature, covered almost invariably with inch-wide, many-petaled, blush-pink blossoms, 'Rouletii' is unarguably good breeding stock. It also makes a phenomenal houseplant, sturdy and productive. It doesn't demand much space, and it defies mildew, black spot, and all the other plagues on roses. It has even proved itself hardy when I mistakenly left a pot outdoors until midwinter. For fortitude alone, 'Rouletii' has always been my favorite. Joy, however, was lukewarm on 'Rouletii.' Indeed, she didn't avail herself of any rose but 'Rosette' for flower-arranging purposes. Her clientele wasn't apt to swoon over a discreet dappling of color in an arrangement anyway. Long before anyone else was playing with uncompromising shades, Joy was harmonizing blazing oranges and fire-engine reds. Our town didn't know it, but we were way ahead of our time.

Of course, both Joy and Uncle Richard would sell you absolutely anything, if only you expressed an interest. But, having been brought up as a florist from the time she could clutch a bunch of violets, Joy always had an affinity for cut flowers. As for Uncle Richard, well, he liked anything that could spark a good story. And yet I always thought it indicative of the orientation he shared with his sister that he invariably stuck a corsage pin or two in the brim of his cap. Customers who came through the door for their anniversary bouquets probably never noticed those corsage pins. You could only really see them when he dozed, greenhouse cat on his lap, head resting softly on his chest.

Rosa 'Peace'

MICHELE AND JEAN-CLAUDE LAMONTAGNE

'La Rose de la Paix'

⌐

(TRANSLATED BY WAYNE WINTERROWD)

IN THE SPACE OF HALF A CENTURY, 'Mme Antoine Meilland' has become the most famous and without doubt the most widely cultivated of roses throughout the world. But the history of the rose is as astonishing as its immense global success. Beautiful, elegant of form, with large, perfectly fashioned blossoms of canary yellow shaded at the edges with warm pink, this rose also possesses exceptional qualities of vigor, resistance to diseases, and adaptability to a very wide range of climatic conditions. It has played an essential part in the story of the rose in our day, and has become the mother of many of our best modern cultivars.

But let us go back to the year 1935, and to a small village near Lyon called Tassin-la-Demi-Lune. There, Francis Meilland, a young rosarian—only twenty-three years old—worked in his trial gardens in constant search of new varieties. He was the descendant of four generations of rose breeders, and his knowledge conjoined with happy accident to lead him to a glorious discovery. He had chosen as female parent an unnamed seedling that contained in its genes four named varieties: 'George Dickson,' a red rose bred in 1912; 'Souvenir de Claudius Pernet,' a yellow rose developed in 1926; 'Joanna Hill,' a yellow with an orange heart from 1928; and 'Charles P. Kilham,' an orange-red hybrid tea developed in 1926. The pollen parent was to be the beautiful yellow rose with superb foliage named 'Margaret McGredy,' bred in 1927. The union of this rose with the unnamed seedling represented a hybrid mix of varieties bred in America, Ireland, and France, truly an international parentage.

Four years later, after he selected from among all the young seedlings that had issued from this cross, fifty remained, and Francis Meilland chose to propagate and distribute number 40, which was then designated simply as "3-35-40." Cuttings were taken from it and distributed to friends and clients throughout Europe, chiefly in Germany and Italy. But in the year 1939, one could sense war coming, and very shortly, communications between the Meilland family and rose growers in both countries were cut off, leaving Francis without news of the fate of his rose. Nevertheless, rosarians in Germany and Italy were enthralled by the roses produced from these cuttings, and in each country a name was assigned. In that time of violence and death, in Italy the rose was called 'Gioia' (Joy), and in Germany it was christened 'Gloria Dei' (Glory of God). Both names have been passed down to our day, though the Meilland family heard of neither until after 1944. But in the meantime, Francis and his father, Antoine, were equally convinced of the exceptional qualities of their creation, and baptized it in 1941 as 'Mme Antoine Meilland,' after their wife and mother, who died quite young in 1932. A remarkable woman, and the daughter of a long line of distinguished rosarians, she was thus honored by a rose that has often been called "the rose of the century."

But the extraordinary history of the rose does not stop there. In 1942, German troops invaded the "Zone Libre" that comprised the southern half of France, including the region around Lyon. George Wittinghill, the U.S. consul based in Lyon and a friend of the Meillands, was forced to leave quite suddenly for home. Francis requested him to transport a few cuttings of 'Mme Antoine Meilland' to the great American rosarian Robert Pyle. Wittinghill agreed, and a packet of five cuttings of "3-35-40" were delivered into the hands of Pyle, who, using his great skill, succeeded in rooting them.

Several weeks after the liberation of France, Francis Meilland received a long-delayed letter from his American correspondent. "I am stunned with admiration for this huge yellow rose shaded with carmine," Pyle wrote. "It is before me, majestic, full of promise, and I am already certain it will be the greatest rose of this century." He further announced that officials of the American Rose Society had also been overwhelmed by the beauty of the rose and at the convention of the Pacific Rose Society in Pasadena had proposed to name it 'Peace.' By a strange wink of history, the baptism of "3-35-40" with this new name occurred on April 29, 1945, the day of the fall of Berlin.

'Peace' took on further symbolic significance on May 8, 1945, the day Germany signed its surrender. The forty-nine delegates to the international conference charged with creating the constitution of what was to become the United Nations all found on their desks a bud of 'Peace' with a message from the secretary of the American Rose Society: "Let this rose influence all men of good will to establish forever peace in the world." In 2005, when the United Nations celebrates its fiftieth anniversary, 'Peace' will certainly be part of the ceremonies. Born in wartime, having escaped the furious destruction of men, this is a rose that carries a message of hope, and its remarkable persistence in dark times makes it as sure a symbol of life as the dove that carried an olive branch to Noah.

But whether we call this rose 'Mme Antoine Meilland' (as perhaps we should) or 'Gioia,' or 'Gloria Dei,' or 'Peace,' there is good reason for its propagation all over the world, and its conquest of an immense number of admirers. It has received the highest prizes, and it has also known an almost unbelievable success among gardeners. In part its popularity is due to its extraordinary color, new in its day, which is a clear yellow overwashed with pinkish orange. But the form of its flower is the perfect rose in many eyes, large and beautiful and wavy of petal. Then, too, its leaves are large, a brilliant green, and of good health. And it blooms and reblooms, even in the absence of pruning or other care.

The exceptional vigor of this rose has also been a strong component of its celebrity. It has what is called in French *rusticité*, which is translated as "hardiness" but means a little more than that—toughness, perhaps. The ability to live on its own and to resist diseases. Ruggedness. It was this quality that brought new life to the hybrid teas that now enrich our gardens. Still, the excellent constitution of the rose would have been of little use had not 'Mme Antoine Meilland' possessed yet another quality precious to rose breeders, its extraordinary fertility. It has served, over almost fifty years of rose breeding, both as seed and pollen parent to a huge number of modern tea roses that dramatically increase the range and vitality of the roses we grow.

MICHELE AND
JEAN-CLAUDE
LAMONTAGNE

In its typical bush form, 'Mme Antoine Meilland' is now cultivated throughout the world, with perhaps the total number of plants in many millions. It looks splendid in large drifts, but it has also given rise to a climbing form that can reach nine feet, thus making it a perfect choice to train against fences or over pergolas. It is also sumptuous when grafted as a tree rose, to a height of perhaps three feet from the ground, in which form it will offer a superb bouquet of flowers at a height of about five feet.

'Mme Antoine Meilland' has been selected by gardeners throughout the world as one of their favorite roses. Its history and beauty inspired the English novelist Antonia Ridge to write *For Love of a Rose* (1965); the House of Meilland in turn named a magnificent red rose after her. So, in a quite curious way, 'La Rose de la Paix'—once simply "3-35-40"—continues its history among us truly like the heroine of a novel.

The immense success of 'Mme Antoine Meilland' virtually guaranteed the success of the small family business directed by Francis Meilland, which subsequently became the House of Meilland. Soon after the war, it occurred to him to separate the results of his research into two branches, one concerned with garden roses, and the other with roses destined for the cut-flower market. Until then, rose hybridists had not taken much account of the fact that those two uses required quite different characteristics in a rose.

In the last half-century, the House of Meilland has produced magnificent roses for the garden, most notably 'Christian Dior,' 'White Knight,' and 'Maria Callas.' More recently, there has been the famous 'Bonica,' bred in 1984, the coppery-pink petals of which—with abundant repeat bloom, healthy foliage, and remarkable vigor—constituted a breakthrough in rose breeding by representing the first "landscape rose." It was followed by 'Carefree Delight,' 'Pierre de Ronsard,'

'Eden Climber,' and 'Cherry Delight.' Many of these have received the prestigious All America Rose Selection (AARS) designation, which recognizes the finest results of rose breeding worldwide.

But one should not forget that the House of Meilland has also bred superb roses to grow under glass for the cut-flower trade, notably 'Baccará,' the cut rose of the 1950s, and then 'Sonia,' which appeared twenty years later and quickly became *the* florist's rose, millions of stems of which are sold throughout the world. There has also been 'Leonidas,' named after the famous Belgian chocolate firm of Greek origin, a rose one can offer even to a gentleman, with its curious tints of tobacco and bitter chocolate. Or 'Black Baccará,' which without doubt is as close as we have yet come to the chimera of a true "black rose." In this way, the long tradition of the House of Meilland has continued through six generations to the present day.

Rosa 'Martin Frobisher'

DAN HINKLEY

Rosa rugosa

FIRST OF ALL, I do not wish to impart to the reader the faintest scent of accomplishment in my growing roses of any kind, including *Rosa rugosa*. For I confess that, even in the most charitable of judgments, my career as a rosarian could be viewed more as out-and-out torment than as a success. Second, I must testify to my contempt for the rose in general, and in particular for that boxwood-framed asylum, the "rose garden." I lack the genius to add my criticisms to a group of shrubs that has accumulated among gardeners more than a trickle of articulate detractors—my caviling would be a poor substitute for their genuine talent at disparaging The Rose. But among the ranks of the vastly overbred and chemically dependent, if there is one rose that defies my disdain for the entire group, it is *Rosa rugosa*. That is a rose that I could learn to respect if I could learn to grow it well.

In 1784, when *Rosa rugosa* set sail from the shores of Japan, it suffered from a confusion of nomenclature, or possibly a bad translation. First collected and described by the Swedish botanist Carl Peter Thunberg (1743–1828), it began cultivation in the West under the name Ramanas Rose—a meaningless misspelling that still adheres to it like lint in modern references. In actuality, the Japanese called this brambly shrub *hama-nasu*, literally "shore pear." It thickly colonizes the salty sands of their beaches, and when its plumped, burnished orbs of fruit ripen in late summer, their vernacular name seems infused with the essence of Japanese delicacy. Beyond the shorelines of Japan, the shore pear also mantles the peninsular beaches of Korea, as well as the climatically brutalized seacoasts of Kamchatka, Sakhalin, and northeastern China. There it thrives in a blasty habitat of frigid temperatures, sodium-chlorinated winds, and beggared soils. Its preferred habitat is actually dry, cold soils—sands even—that are sharp and infertile. If fêted with an enriched soil and generous moisture, *Rosa rugosa* may heap resentment upon you like compost after autumn cleanup.

There is much to be said for toughness in a garden plant. But durability for the mere sake of durability in a rose can result in an embittered tangle of thorny stems that refuse to die. Even in a rose, one naturally expects more than that. The *rugosa*s offer much more, certainly, and their excellent qualities may be summed up in four words: foliage, stems, flower, and fruit. Let us take these words in turn.

Foliage first. To begin with, it is deep green, and when it is the color it should be (and refuses to be in my own present garden), it seems almost the black-green of an agitated sea. The texture of the leaflet surface is the cheek of a lean, field-laboring Siberian, taut but patterned with the lines of wind and weather, a characteristic grain that accounts for the rose's Latin species designation, *rugosa*, signifying "wrinkled." This chlorophyllic signature reveals *rugosa* blood in the leaves of hybrid generations far removed from its wild, seaside origins. "Oh, that's a *rugosa*," one might easily say, even in the dark in late spring before flowers have appeared, when nothing but a nocturnal touch reveals the veining etched deeply atop the leaf.

Rosa rugosa took its own sweet time in officially becoming *Rosa rugosa*. In the early decades of the nineteenth century, when it made its real debut in Europe, it passed under the name *Rosa ferox*—*ferox* being the Latin root of the English "ferocious" and, when applied to a plant, meaning "very thorny." This brings us, of course, to the rose's stems. I have known the stems of many rose species, and many species of roses have, in a bloody fashion, known me. With such a cognomen as *ferox*, one might expect the rasping snarl of toothy canes, but *Rosa rugosa* is not that way at all. Resolutely thorny it is, certainly, but its thorns are mere whiskers in comparison with the many barbed brutes with which I have found myself entangled in the wild and the garden alike. The new stems, which should always be encouraged by hard spring pruning, retain a suffusion of burgundy during the winter months, while their hairlike bristles bleach to a tasteful tawny beige. For those who see the more subtle effects of garden plants, it is a pretty combination.

If I were prone to embellishment, I might say that it is not enough to grow and admire *rugosa* roses and occasionally behead one for a vase. The redolence of any rose is a sensation we wish to wallow in, like the sappy, unlikely scenarios of a romantic comedy that ends happily. Elegant and elemental, the scent of *Rosa rugosa*'s flowers is no exception. In China as early as A.D. 1100, the rose's petals were pulverized and its oils blended with musk and camphor, an alchemy meant to preserve the ephemeral fragrance of the flower at its finest moment.

The wild forms collected for this mélange proffered delicate, silky petals of a spirited magenta-red, with a prominent central boss of golden stamens. But the development of the wild forms to their current state of domesticated refinement is comparable to that of the evolution of early anthropoids to the contemporary leader of the free world, a distance considerably shorter than to that of modern humans. Over hundreds of years, the keen eyes of collectors in the gardening cultures of both China and Japan found numerous naturally occurring forms of the species, which is actually quite variable in the wild. Those forms, extracted from Nature herself, ultimately provided the basis for modern breeding and selection.

The lineage of most modern garden *rugosa* roses is complicated, especially since this species possesses the procreative scruples of a rabbit in estrus. When the rose is put in proximity to virtually any other rose species, its predisposition toward indiscriminate engagement results in abundant hybrid progeny. In fact, even before *Rosa rugosa* was introduced into gardens and the hands of breeders, hybrids had occurred spontaneously in its natural habitats. *Rosa* × *iwara*, for example, results frequently wherever the natural range of *Rosa rugosa* overlaps that of another predominantly Japanese species, *Rosa multiflora*. The sad results may be an uncomely congregation of dead-end chromosomes devoid of the genes responsible for beauty. Nature does not always do things better than humans, though we like to think so.

Yet, like the apple, *Rosa rugosa* willingly pleased the Western world, intent as we have been on creating, for fun and profit, new forms of plants from all the genotypes of the earth. No rose is more generous than *Rosa rugosa* at parenting, and though most of the resulting panoply of mongrels have deserved the bonfire, many forms and hybrids with the vigorous *Rosa rugosa* blood have been perpetuated by gardeners. Surviving still are the 'Grootendorsts' and 'Gravereauxs,' the 'Blancs Doubles de Coubert,' the 'Belles Poitevines,' and dozens more whose euphonious names alone seem to justify their existence.

We don't know how frequently *Rosa rugosa* was grown for the first hundred years after its introduction into Europe in 1784, or how much it was appreciated. What is known is that when it was rereleased in the late nineteenth century, under the name *Rosa regeliana*, commemorating Her Royal Dourness, Queen Victoria, it was embraced with fervor. In fact, and quite remarkably, the elegant purity of *Rosa rugosa*'s single flowers temporarily diverted Victorian rose-breeding from the reigning cabbagelike ideal. To this day, many of the best forms of *Rosa rugosa* remain single selections of the undiluted species itself, a rather bold statement considering the species' proclivity toward genetic mingling. One never can know for sure. But the best *rugosa* roses simply *look* like *rugosa* roses.

Take, for example, the famous 'Fru Dagmar Hastrup' (often 'Hartopp,' though it is marketed both ways). This rose has a delicious, wafery bundling of pastel pink with all of the *rugosas*' inherent easiness—the same unassuming easiness one loves in silver-bleached seaside rental cottages whose kitchens have mixed and chipped coffee mugs and World's Fair souvenirs on the corner shelves. *Rosa rugosa* 'Alba' remains the finest in foliage, flower, and fruit, with a clarity of white petal almost unique in the plant kingdom, and a delicious perfume strewn about a rounded mound of fine, rugose green leaves and dependable scarlet fruits.

The single-flowered forms of known hybrid origin are very numerous. However, one stands above the lot, not for its abundant, pink-drenched, tartly fragrant blossoms or its fine leaves of glazed green (all of which are fine enough), but for its curious and convoluted evolution into an entirely new rose species. 'Max Graf' resulted from a pairing between *Rosa rugosa* and the prostrate-growing *Rosa wichuraiana*, and as with all other *Rosa rugosa* hybrids, it seemed to be a sterile mule. But after repeated breeding attempts, 'Max Graf' produced three seedlings, one of which proved to be a tetraploid, and completely fertile. It was named *Rosa kordesii* to commemorate Wilhelm Kordes, the great German rose-breeder—a name under which, thanks to its returning to complete fertility, it has been granted the status of a true species.

Later, when *Rosa kordesii* was back-crossed to *Rosa rugosa*, the resulting progeny served in Felicitas Svejda's remarkable breeding programs, sponsored by the Canadian Department of Agriculture in the 1980s. From her work, the highly regarded Explorer and Parkland series—all stalwartly hardy—came to the aid of the climatically assaulted Northern gardener. Named after early explorers of Canada, her numerous crosses resulted in such notable roses as the single, blush-white 'Henry Hudson,' the clear red, clustered 'John Cabot,' and the deep-pink 'William Baffin.' Among her great triumphs was also 'Martin Frobisher,' with clusters of numerous candy-pink buds fading to the palest pink at their edges, and open flowers so faint a pink that it might rather be called some lovely shade of white. Grown on their own roots, these roses can retreat to ground level during particularly nasty winters, even in frigid USDA Zone 4, and regrow to become bountiful with blossom by summer's end.

The many double-flowered hybrids of *Rosa rugosa* are lovely—though, as always when you multiply petal count, you must decide how exactly to rid yourself of the disgusting brown mélange into which the flowers degenerate after blooming. 'Blanc Double de Coubert' is an exception, an uncorrupted confection with a tantalizing semi-doubling of white petals, and a superb scent. The doubling effect, however, is carried too far in 'Souvenir de Philémon Cochet' and company, when flowers no longer are composed of petals but instead become a sort of pulpy affectation.

Selections and hybrids of *Rosa rugosa* possess long seasons of both flowering and ripening fruit, so the two functions—flower and fruit—often overlap and interplay. But long after flowering has ceased and the foliage has briefly assumed its autumn tones of tawny yellow and beige, the hips remain, colored the dull orange of baked pumpkin, or the glistening Christmas red of a freshly sliced pomegranate.

In late autumn, a naked sweep of three . . . fifteen . . . forty-five or more *Rosa rugosa*s, broken here and there with skeletal shafts of grasses, mud flats swelling with a high tide in the fore, a flock of cranes taking wing above, white pines with horizontal planes of blue-green in the distance—these are the elements of a Japanese woodblock print by Hiroshiga, both delicious and predictable.

On a high precipice over Puget Sound, in ample light that might be considered a full blister of sun by those who live in the Pacific Northwest, I have again begun to chart the course of a garden. In the sandy and impotent soil of the bluff, *Rosa rugosa* 'Blanc Double de Coubert' was one of the first shrubs I planted. I brought it from my original garden at Heronswood, where it had languished for nearly fifteen years. I brought it here to stabilize the soil of this ledge, and in only months it has responded, with the green of health and dozens of dazzling white flowers that float amidst the sparkle of water in the distance. And, with a few more seasons to brag of, in a garden that can actually grow *rugosa* roses well, I just may be able to tell you why I like them so much. Assuredly, my growing affections will come by way of summer flowers and foliage, as well as their thorny stems and decorous fruit, poised upon the dormant winter landscape.

Rosa gallica officinalis

FERGUS GARRETT

The Turkish Rose

⤙

I N ONE WAY OR ANOTHER, the rose is featured in many of the wonderful stories associated with love and romance in Turkish history, lore, and myth, relayed over the centuries by poets and historians. The rose is the essence of purity, sweetness, and femininity. An admiring lover will often affix the word *gül* (meaning "rose") to his sweetheart's name as a term of affection. He may describe her complexion as being as fair as a rose, or her skin as being soft as a rose petal. Dreaming of roses signifies an improvement in one's love life, health, and general well-being. Rose petals were stuffed into silken mattresses for the ultimate seductive experience. But love never comes without a price, and romance and tragedy often go hand in hand in Turkish lore. One old saying particularly comes to mind: "You cannot pluck roses without the fear of thorns, nor enjoy a fair wife without the danger of horns."

Along with the carnation and the tulip, the rose is an important flower in Turkish art and culture. Rose motifs are found on the garments of the sultans, on Iznik pottery, on carpets, and on copperware. Roses also feature prominently in Turkey's rich and varied cuisine. For centuries the rose's delightful scent has been captured by infusing petals in water, oil, honey, and sugar to flavor drinks, puddings, and sweets. The tradition lives on today, most notably in the rose flavoring of Turkish Delight.

Turkey, rich in plants generally, has over twenty native species of rose. This includes *Rosa gallica*, the ancestor of many beautiful garden hybrids, as well as culinary roses such as the damasks that are so popular in Turkish kitchens. *Rosa gallica* was named by Linnaeus, who assumed that it had originated in Roman Gaul. In fact, the species stretches from Central to Southern Europe through to Iraq. It is found throughout Turkey in dry meadows and maquis, in dunes, and sometimes on pure sand. A low shrub growing up to three feet with stiff, upright, densely prickled stems, and dull, bluish-green leaves, *Rosa gallica* bears masses of strongly scented, deep-pink, solitary flowers followed by scarlet-orange hips. Naturally occurring hybrids of this rose are distributed throughout Europe and Western Asia.

Although *Rosa gallica* has a fainter scent than the damask roses, its petals possess the amazing virtue of retaining fragrance even after they wither. This means that they can be dried and made into scented powder, and then used in salves, oils, and rose-scented waters. Thought to possess many medicinal properties, rose potions are frequently referred to in ancient texts. Military doctors took *Rosa gallica* on campaigns, planting it whenever possible. With the ability to produce copious amounts of seed, sucker underground, and tolerate extremes of heat and cold in different habitats, the highly fertile *gallica* thrived in military outposts, monasteries, and gardens, spreading throughout the East and Europe. Selection and breeding gave rise to many variants. A highly fragrant, semi-double form of the species was selected and became the favored rose of apothecaries. This rose of legendary medicinal properties is known today as *Rosa gallica officinalis*, the Apothecary's Rose. Its quality was so superior that it initiated an entire industry dedicated to its medicinal and confectionary uses.

Rosa damascena, whose origin has been subject to much debate, is thought to be a hybrid of *R. gallica* and *R. phoenicia*. *R. phoenicia* is found in southern and western Turkey in scrubby, moist places. It is a stoutly prickled climbing shrub growing up to fifteen feet high, with white to pale-pink flowers borne on dense corymbs and possessed of a musky scent. Crossing this rose with *Rosa gallica* resulted in a very floriferous shrubby plant with an irresistibly rich scent. The pale-pink flowers borne in clusters carry a mixture of essential oils from both parents, giving them an unmistakable strong fragrance that lasts through processing. These qualities have made the summer-flowering damask rose *R. damascena*, also known as the Isparta Rose, world-renowned for the production of rose oil and rose water. A variant, *R. damascena* 'Trigintipetala,' the "thirty-petaled" or Kazanlik rose, has the semi-double *Rosa gallica officinalis* as one of its parents. The resulting hybrid has such an abundance of petals, and such a delicious rich scent, that it has become the favored rose of growers in Turkey.

Rose oil, produced by steam-distilling freshly picked flowers, is called "attar" of roses, the name derived from an Arabic word meaning "fragrant." The distilling process is thought to have originated in Mogul India, where a means of separating the water and the essential oil was accidentally discovered at a banquet given by the Emperor Jahangir (1605–1627). His rosewater-filled pools underwent a natural distillation in the heat of the sun, which left a thin film of oil floating on the surface that was found to have a lasting perfume. The Ottoman Turks developed the distillation process, and with the spread of their empire, which was to last for more than five hundred years, introduced it to many provinces. Today, Turkey and the once Ottoman-occupied Bulgaria are the most important producers of attar of roses. The two main centers of cultivation are in Kazanluk (from the Turkish *kazan*, meaning "still"), in Bulgaria, and the Isparta district of Turkey, in southwestern Anatolia.

Over 60 percent of the world's production of the highest-quality oil takes place in Turkey. Most of the roses are grown in small, family-owned farms. Picking starts at sunrise and is completed in the morning. The harvest is then rushed to the stills, and the distillation is done on the same day. The process involves passing steam over the petals and then condensing the steam into large bottles, which yields mainly fragrant rose water, but also a thin layer of rose oil. It takes more than four tons of flowers to produce a kilo of oil, which is worth literally its weight in gold. The first and second distillations are blended before being packed in wax-sealed copper canisters and exported all over the world, including the famous perfumeries of Grasse, in southern France.

Go to any decent Turkish garden today and you'll see pink roses grown for the kitchen. More than likely, the species will be the Isparta Rose, *Rosa damascena*, or a close relative such as the Kazanlik, or possibly *Rosa centifolia*, the cabbage rose, known in Turkey as the *Okka gülü*. Whatever the species, it will be highly scented, and rich in essential oils. My mother swears by her Isparta roses tucked on either side of the main gate of our house in the coastal resort of Yalova, across the Sea of Marmara from Istanbul. The roses came with us from our last house in Istanbul, and probably from the house before that, cherished and preserved like a valuable piece of furniture. My great-grandmother used them, followed by my late grandmother, and now they are in the possession of my mother, who will then pass them on to me, and I on to my children. And, believe me, they are the real thing, for I have tasted the rose-petal jam that my mother lovingly produces from them year after year, following an old family recipe. This is a delicate breakfast jam to be eaten on fresh bread or toast.

Nebahat Hanim's Rose Petal Jam

1½ pounds (650 grams) fresh rose petals

9½ cups (1950 grams) superfine sugar

Juice of 1 lemon

2½ cups (750 ml) fresh spring water

1 egg white

Wash the rose petals, and snip off and reserve their white bases. Alternately layer the petals and half of the sugar in a bowl, then pour the lemon juice over, reserving 2 teaspoons. Cover the bowl with a cloth and set aside.

Place the white tips of the rose petals into a separate bowl, boil the water, and pour 2½ cups boiling water on top. Cover with a damp cloth, and set aside. Let both bowls rest at cool room temperature for two days.

After two days, gently stir the sugar-and-rose-petal mixture. Cover again. Drain the liquid from the white petal tips into a saucepan. Add the remaining sugar and the egg white, and bring to a boil. Simmer, skimming off the froth, until you are left with a clear syrup.

Add the sugared rose petals and return to a simmer, again spooning off the froth. When the mixture starts to darken, add the remaining 2 teaspoons of lemon juice, then remove from heat. Let the jam cool for a few minutes, then put it into sterilized jars and seal.

This essay would not be complete without mentioning aşure (pronounced "ash-ur-ey"), a legendary sweet flavored with rose water and also known as Noah's Pudding. It contains a list of ingredients as long as your arm and looks like fruits and nuts preserved in aspic. Legend has it that Noah found himself running extremely short of supplies on the ark and ordered that all the remaining food be cooked together. The result turned out to be delicious. In Ottoman times the sweet was consumed in "Aşure month." Modern Turks still make and eat it, but unfortunately the dish is less popular in the kitchens of the young, as it's quite an effort to put together. My mother still makes it, and sends bowls of it to all the neighbors, who return the bowls full of figs, plums, or shortbread cakes. It's a tradition that I will carry on.

AŞURE

⅓ cup (50 grams) dried white beans

⅓ cup (50 grams) dried white lima beans

⅓ cup (50 grams) long-grain rice

⅔ cup (100 grams) wheat or bran flakes

1½ cups (450 milliliters) milk

1 cup plus 2 tablespoons (225 grams) sugar

⅔ cup (100 grams) chopped pitted dates

½ cup (75 grams) blanched whole almonds

½ cup (125 milliliters) rose water

Seeds of 1 pomegranate

⅓ cup (50 grams) currants

⅔ cup (100 grams) raisins

⅓ cup (50 grams) chopped walnuts

3 tablespoons (25 grams) pine nuts

Additional raisins, walnuts, and pomegranate seeds for garnish

Soak the dried white beans and dried white lima beans overnight. Boil them in separate saucepans until tender, about 1 hour. Drain them, and allow them to cool.

Boil the rice and wheat or bran flakes in separate saucepans in plenty of water, until they are tender. Strain them, reserving the water in which they were cooked. Chop coarsely.

Place a little more than one quart (1.2 liters) of the water used for cooking the rice and wheat in a saucepan. Add milk and sugar and bring to a boil, stirring until the sugar is fully dissolved. Boil until the mixture thickens enough to coat a spoon, then add all the other ingredients except garnishes. Boil for 2 or 3 minutes more and remove from heat. Pour into individual cups and allow to cool.

Serve cold in individual cups decorated with raisins, walnut halves, and pomegranate seeds.

Rosa 'Königin von Dänemark.'

PAMELA STAGG

'Königin von Dänemark'

IS IT POSSIBLE TO FALL IN LOVE with a face in a photograph? For a romantic like me, absolutely! That's what happened with 'Königin von Dänemark.'

I wasn't looking for romance that day, only a book—any book—that could help me deal with the garden my then-husband and I had just bought. I, who had never gardened before, was enchanted with the generous garden around the New England–style house we had chosen. My husband, who *had* gardened before, made me promise—before we made an offer on the property—that I would look after all the gardening. I gave him my word, and after a short, tense bidding war, the place was ours, from the underinsulated roof to the collapsed wall in the basement. The garden was in equally sad shape. I estimated, from the hundreds of knee-high maples out back, that the elderly former owner had been incapacitated for about three years. The flower beds had disappeared under weeds and lawn; only the odd peony, rose, or iris hinted at their location. As someone whose sole experience with plants was a window box of basil and geraniums, I was totally daunted by the practical realities of the garden.

While we worked on the kitchen, the bathroom, and the front porch, I watched the contract gardeners in the neighborhood. They used peat moss to amend the soil. Clearly, peat moss was the way to go. So I went to the local garden center and bought what I thought was a very large bag of peat moss.

Actually, it turned out to be a small bag. A very small bag.

And for a city property, my garden was big. Very big.

My first day in the garden, it became obvious that my small bag of peat moss and my even smaller knowledge of horticulture were totally inadequate to the task of rescuing the sad, neglected garden.

So I did what anyone from an academic family does. I headed for a bookshop.

That's when I first saw 'Königin von Dänemark' ("Queen of Denmark"), on the cover of a book about old roses by Trevor Griffith. It was unlike any rose I'd ever seen, with a button center and beautiful soft pink petals curved around a central axis in the quartered arrangement that was to become so familiar to me. Once, in a poem, I had come across the phrase "the architecture of a flower." That seemed a perfect description for the elegant arrangement of 'Königin von Dänemark's' petals. It was love at first sight. I *had* to have that rose.

It was my good fortune that one of the best rose nurseries on the continent was close to my home. Within days, I was poring over the Pickering Nurseries catalogue, where I found ideal companions for 'Königin von Dänemark,' historic roses with wonderful names like Father Hugo's rose, *Rosa mundi*, and 'Camieux.' I sent in my order, and the roses arrived on a bitterly cold fall day. I still remember how my hands felt as if they would shatter as I dug the dormant plants into their new home.

The next spring, I waited eagerly for my new roses to emerge. I was in for a treat. Not only does 'Königin von Dänemark' have a beautiful face, she also has some of the most beautiful leaves in the rose family, a soft blue-green with a matte finish that's a wonderful backdrop for other plants. And then came the flowers, every bit as beautiful as the photograph had promised. And the scent was enchanting.

The following summer, I decided to expand my knowledge of roses. I took a course at a botanical garden with an excellent rose garden, and under the guidance of George Pagowski, the extremely knowledgeable rosarian there, I met, in the flesh, many of the roses to which the Pickering Nurseries catalogue had introduced me. There were huge beds of *rugosa*s, *alba*s, shrub roses, Chinas, Portlands, species roses, early hybrid teas—an exhaustive collection.

I made two discoveries during that course. First, I loved old roses; and, second, there was nothing—for me—that could come close to the beauty of 'Königin von Dänemark.' Compared with the lanky growth of, say, 'York and Lancaster,' 'Königin von Dänemark' had a graceful shape that looked as wonderful in the winter months as in the summer. Next to the *rugosa*s she had a limited number of thorns, so I wouldn't be picking splinters from my hands for two days after pruning, as I do after I work on my *rugosa* hedge. The leaves seemed to be the definitive rose leaves, attractive in their own right yet also a wonderful foil for the flowers. And those blooms—soft pink, richly petaled, and quartered—spoke of cloistered medieval gardens and intricate illustrations in old manuscripts. Finally, there was the scent, which few modern roses can match.

After seeing those other roses, I wouldn't have traded my 'Königin von Dänemark' for all the tea roses in China.

That fall, I did a very bad thing.

I decided not to provide winter mulch for some of the roses in the garden—the modern hybrid teas I tentatively identified as 'Tropicana.'

They died. (No surprise.)

So I planted more old roses in their place.

And when a group of shrubs succumbed to an obscure disease a few years later, I created another bed for old roses. Though most of them were new to the garden—'Bullata,' 'Crested Moss,' and 'Mme Pierre Oger'—a new 'Königin von Dänemark' bush was given pride of place.

Time has passed, and a generation of cats lies buried under the white peonies beside the patio where little Alyssa plays lazily with Ghost's tail.

My first 'Königin von Dänemark' is now a handsome, elegantly shaped shrub, a pleasure to look at even in the depths of winter. This spring, it was simply covered in blooms so fragrant that I could never walk past without pausing to enjoy them. The garden has grown, to my great surprise, into something very attractive to me and to my neighbors. In an area where a number of gardens seem to consist of only seven significant shrubs and a piece of granite, it charms people with its profuse flowers, especially in June, when the irises, peonies, and roses are in bloom.

When my property was chosen for a garden tour last year, many visitors commented on the work that must have gone into it. Yes, there were many years of hard physical labor and many hours spent studying gardening books and magazines, and taking courses. There were horticultural experiments, like the espaliered apricot on the south wall of the garage and a vigorous rooted cutting of an extremely ugly shrub (now composted) that was homework for a plant-propagation course. There were other failures, too, like the "hardy" cyclamen and *Iris reticulata* that couldn't stand the cold. There was damage inflicted by the neighbor's dog, who bounced through a bed of rare young plants. And there were also ice storms, devastating snowstorms, seasons of drought, and seasons of unseasonable cold that took their toll on me, and the garden. There was a year when I had whooping cough, and three difficult years when I was injured and could do virtually nothing in the garden. Since I didn't trust the neighborhood contract gardeners—who seem to reduce every shrub to a box or a ball—'Königin von Dänemark' got no pruning, no fertilizer, and no detergent spray to control the caterpillars that are such a pest here in Toronto.

You would never know that, looking at her now.

It is often said that a true lover never reveals the faults of the beloved. 'Königin von Dänemark' has suffered my neglect graciously, never complaining about my treatment with restrained growth or scanty blooms. All through the difficult years—and in all the years since—she has remained lovely and free-flowering.

And I, lover that I am, can only say that if 'Königin von Dänemark' has a fault I have yet to discover it.

She remains, for me, the perfect rose.

Rosa
'Ballerina'

Rosa
glauca

Rosa
'Heritage'

Rosa
centifolia
'Cristata'

Rosa
pimpinellifolia

Rosa
rugosa

Rosa
moyesii

Rose Hips

JOE ECK

Rose Hips

⁓

IN THE GENUS *ROSA*, which contains more than one hundred species and tens of thousands of cultivars, there are roses worth growing for every reason imaginable. Certainly there is the beauty of the flowers, which are almost infinite in color and form. There is the decadent scent of many, and the air of romance that hangs about even their names—'Coupe d'Hébé,' 'Variegata di Bologna,' 'Great Maiden's Blush,' *Rosa mundi*, and so on. But beyond these obvious and celebrated attributes are qualities less often noted but just as valuable in the garden. *Rosa glauca*, for example, possesses foliage as arresting as that of any purple cotinus. Others offer autumn tints as warm and russet as those of a fothergilla or a vaccinium, and still others, fruits as jewel-like as those of a callicarpa or a holly. *Rosa omeinesis* var. *pteracantha* possesses scarlet thorns that are as beautiful to look at as they are plentiful and painful to touch. Often these leaves, thorns, and fruits grace the garden in August, September, and October, when there may be little else to see, when we—and the garden—need a little cheering up.

Setting thorns and foliage aside, the fruits (or hips) of roses are among the mainstays of the late-autumn and early-winter garden. When all else has passed, when the last leaves have been blown from the trees and thick snow is on the ground, many rose hips still glisten. Among my favorites is a venerable cultivar with the engagingly sturdy name of 'Old Red Moss.' Though its younger stems bear a number of small, sharp brown bristles that indicate its heritage and account for its classification among the mosses, the rose itself is not very mossy. The plant produces a profusion of cherry-colored semi-double flowers in June, but it earns its place in the garden as much for its copious and long-lasting hips. These rich, dark, burnished red fruits are about an inch in circumference and cling to the stems well into January. The plant seldom grows taller than four feet, but it is apt to become a little stout with age, and so benefits from a corset of weathered wood, which both reins it in and enhances its name, making it seem as if it tumbled over a derelict fragment of homestead fence.

Rosa glauca, admired all summer for its strangely beautiful smoky-purple foliage, claims attention again in autumn for its hips. These are oval in shape and similar to a ripe cranberry in size and color, which makes sprays of them splendid for early-autumn bouquets. They occur in clusters of a dozen or so, and are quite prominent after the foliage has fallen away, but they tend to drop from the bush by late November. Most of the fallen ones are spirited away by mice; in the spring we sometimes find their cozy nests lined with the seed. But there are always a few volunteer seedlings beneath the bush or about the garden that are worth transplanting and growing on, or giving away. Because it is a species, *Rosa glauca* comes true from seed.

By far the most fruitful of roses is *Rosa rugosa*, called the beach rose for its capacity to flourish in seemingly barren sand. Although it is a Japanese species, it has naturalized widely along the New England seacoast and is a first choice among roses—and, indeed, among all other shrubs—for windswept spots. *Rosa rugosa* blooms all summer and well into the autumn. It and most of its hybrids are easily recognized by their thick, healthy green leaves and by their large, globe-shaped hips. Because *R. rugosa* sets its fruits quickly, the gardener can enjoy the delightful conjunction of five-inch flowers in shades of rich pink (or white, in the forms 'Alba' and 'Blanc Double de Coubert') against the clear bright red of the hips. After flowers and leaves have passed, the clusters of hips linger deep into autumn, until several frosts have made them palatable to hungry birds. The fruits look something like diminutive tomatoes in form and color, but humans find them far too acidic to eat straight from the bush. They must first be made into jelly, which is excellent and very high in vitamin C.

Among the best roses for hips is *Rosa eglanteria*, a species that rivals the most romantically named French hybrid rose in its historical and poetic associations. It is the sweetbrier of English hedgerows, and it provided Chaucer with the name of his refined and flirtatious prioress in *The Canterbury Tales* ("And she was cleped madame Eglentyne"). The sweetbrier, or eglantine, is worth growing for many reasons. It is a stately plant, reaching eight or more feet quickly and preserving a vaselike shape thickly congested with yellowish-green thorny stems, an almost impenetrable barrier to human or beast. Its single pink flowers, about two inches across, have an engaging innocence about them, though they will shatter quickly if picked. The foliage, too, is remarkable for its faint fresh scent of roses, most apparent after a summer shower. But its hips are its greatest glory. They are borne in rich abundance in loose panicles. Each hip is about three-quarters of an inch long, a bright orange-yellow. Whereas many rose hips lose much of their color after a sequence of hard freezes, those of the eglantine remain bright all winter long and even into early spring.

Equally associated with the hedgerows of the English countryside, though certainly less sweetly named, is *Rosa canina*, the Dog Rose. Because it roots easily and forms a very vigorous and thrifty root system, it has long been a favorite among rose growers as an understock on which to graft select hybrid varieties, many of which prove difficult or impossible to root on their own. Gardeners may therefore know it very well as the shoots that sprout from the grafts of choice roses, throwing up lanky, apple-green growth all around more desirable plants. These shoots are aptly called "suckers," and their great vigor enables them to overwhelm a more delicate species or hybrid, eventually annihilating it as they continue to flourish. More than a few gardeners have said to themselves, "My, how well that rose is doing!" only to be greeted eventually by small, single, pale-pink blossoms about two inches across and of brief life, rather than the opulent globes of 'Variegata di Bologna' or 'Cuisse de Nymphe' they were expecting.

But *Rosa canina* also has its place in gardens, not so much for its flower (which is certainly lovely enough for most ordinary purposes) as for its growth habit and its hips. When allowed to become a free-standing bush, it can build up quickly into a stout shrub twelve or fifteen feet tall. That might be nice enough, in the right place. But the species can be very fine indeed when grown up a small tree—an apple tree, for preference. Though its little flowers might pass relatively unnoticed there, in autumn its magnificent hips—again cranberry-sized, in panicles, and of the most vivid, clear red—will not. So it is worth digging out and transplanting a sucker or two of this generally despised species into a shrub border or beneath an apple tree. I have one clambering twenty feet into the splendid old English apple called 'Cox's Orange Pippin,' the late-maturing fruits of which are a scarlet red that exactly matches the hips of the Dog Rose. Whether this is to be considered gilding the apple, or the rose, I have never quite been able to decide.

The hips of most roses come in shades from red to yellow-orange, but those of *Rosa roxburghii* are acid yellow. They are also larger than most rose hips, up to two inches long and three inches in diameter. Each is covered with protective bristles, rather like the outer burr of a chestnut, which has given the plant its common name, the chestnut rose. *Rosa roxburghii* is a large, robust shrub growing to six feet in height and as much in width. It fruits abundantly, and the fruits cling to the branches all autumn long. Older stems and branches develop shredding bark, making the plant, in both bark and burred hip, an altogether striking element of the autumn landscape.

No survey of roses valued for their hips can leave out *Rosa moyesii*. A native of western China, it is curious among roses for several reasons. In some cultivars, particularly the one called 'Geranium,' this rose bears single, two-inch blossoms that are as close to blood red as almost any flower can get. The bush is a sturdy if lanky thing that throws self-supporting canes up to nine feet in height, each of which may be as thick as a broomstick. The general eccentricity of the species is carried to its hips, which can be up to two and a half inches long and are usually described as flask- or bottle-shaped. They preserve most of the true red color of the flowers but are tempered a bit with orange. There are never many hips on the plant, yet the color, size, and shape of those that do appear make them vivid notes in the autumn landscape.

Many gardeners, especially those who live in New England, neglect autumn color when choosing anything except trees for their garden, believing perhaps that Nature's play of beech, birch, and maple is sufficient. But shrubs, and especially some of the shrub roses, sometimes offer wonderful late-season leaf color that holds after the forest has shed its brilliance. Well into November, our garden is bright with the russet oranges and yellows of the species roses, particularly the butter yellow of *Rosa rugosa*, the mahogany red of *R. pimpinellifalia*, and the foliage of the Canadian hybrid *Rosa* 'Metis,' which offers all the colors of autumn—burnt orange and yellow and mahogany and crimson. The leaves of many roses color while still holding their hips, but *Rosa virginiana* adds an occasional three-inch-wide, silver-pink single flower to its impressive autumn display. By October it has set hundreds of small, glossy, holly-bright red hips, among which the flowers nestle against a background of gold to orange leaves. The effect lasts well into the heavy frosts, by which time any skeptic will concede that flowers are not the sole reason to grow roses.

ABOUT THE CONTRIBUTORS

ROSIE ATKINS spent fifteen years working for the *Sunday Times* (London) before becoming a freelance garden writer for various newspapers and magazines. In 1987 she and her family spent a year traveling around the world, which furthered her interest in how other people gardened. In 1992 she started working on the launch of *Gardens Illustrated*, and was the Editor of the magazine for ten years. She left in 2002 to become Curator of the Chelsea Physic Garden in London.

Born in 1926, DAVID AUSTIN has always lived in Shropshire, where he is head of David Austin Roses of Albrighton, a firm that grows more than a thousand varieties of roses and markets worldwide. Famed for his work as a hybridizer, he is the creator of the English Rose, which combines the attributes of antique and old roses with the continuous bloom of modern hybrid teas. His wife is the sculptress Pat Austin, and one of his sons, David, and his daughter, Claire, are both engaged in the firm.

PETER BEALES has been a professional rose-grower since leaving school. He founded Peter Beales Roses in 1968. He lectures worldwide and has so far written three major books on roses. He is currently president of the Royal National Rose Society.

LLOYD BRACE had a gardening mother who took care to enable and encourage all four children in her passion. After MIT, during a business career that began conventionally in the late fifties and ended in advertising in 1990, he gardened for food and landscaping, but never touched roses. A chance late-career apprenticeship in roses set him on the path to establishing The Roseraie in Maine in 1992 and operating for ten seasons a mail-order rose-plant business.

A columnist for *House & Garden* magazine, THOMAS CHRISTOPHER maintains an affection for the gardens of the Old South. His current projects include the re-creation of vintage New England hard ciders.

THOMAS C. COOPER lives and gardens outside of Boston. For twenty-two years the editor of *Horticulture* magazine, then editorial director of *The Gardener* magazine, he is now director of publications for White Flower Farm.

PAGE DICKEY is a gardener, as well as a garden writer and lecturer. Her books include *Duck Hill Journal: A Year in a Country Garden*, *Breaking Ground: Portraits of Ten Garden Designers*, *Inside Out: Relating Garden to House*, *Dogs in Their Gardens*, and *Cats in Their Gardens*.

KEN DRUSE is a regular contributor to *The New York Times*, and an award-winning photographer, writer, and television host. His work has appeared in nearly every home-decorating and gardening magazine as well as in his own best-selling books. He currently gardens behind his studio in Brooklyn, New York, and at his home in northwestern New Jersey.

RORY DUSOIR was brought up in Northern Ireland before being accepted to study classics at Balliol College, Oxford. There he was tutored in ancient history by Oswyn Murray, who also helped to encourage his nascent passion for horticulture, and to whom this contribution is respectfully dedicated. On completing his degree, Mr. Dusoir started his gardening career at Chilcombe House, Dorset, before moving to Great Dixter.

JOE ECK is the author of *The Elements of Garden Design*, and (with Wayne Winterrowd) *A Year at North Hill* and *Living Seasonally*. After taking a degree in philosophy and meeting Wayne, he spent a year in Europe listening to Wagner. On returning to the U.S., he moved to Vermont to raise chickens and to garden. He still does both.

THOMAS FISCHER is the editor of *Horticulture* magazine. He tends a one-quarter-acre garden in Boston, and has published more than 130 articles and reviews.

JANE GARMEY is the author of *The Writer in the Garden, Great British Cooking: A Well-Kept Secret*, and *Great New British Cooking*. She has published articles on gardens, food, travel, and lifestyles and writes a garden column for *Town & Country*.

FERGUS GARRETT is half Turkish and grew up with his mother at their home in Istanbul. He studied horticulture at Wye College (University of London) and has been the head gardener of Christopher Lloyd's garden, Great Dixter, for more than ten years. He is currently on the Royal Horticultural Society's Floral Trials, Floral A, and Dahlia committees. He has lectured throughout the UK and USA and has written many articles. Turkey, its history, culture, and cuisine are of particular interest. Fergus's mother, Nebahat Hanım, still lives in Istanbul where she gardens and is a particularly good cook.

MAC GRISWOLD, who has been writing about gardens and landscape since 1982, gardens in Sag Harbor, New York. Her previous books include *The Golden Age of American Gardens*, written with Eleanor Weller, and *Washington's Gardens at Mount Vernon: Landscape of the Inner Man*. Her most recent book, *Slaves in the Attic: The History of Sylvester Manor, a Long Island Plantation*, grows out of her interest in the makers of the colonial American landscape.

DANIEL J. HINKLEY and his partner, Robert L. Jones, began Heronswood Nursery, near Kingston, Washington, in 1987. Devoted to introducing rare and unusual plants to gardeners of North America, this endeavor has led Hinkley into the wilds of Asia, South America, Mexico, South Africa, and Tasmania. Hinkley writes for numerous periodicals, and his books include *Winter Ornamentals* and *The Explorers Garden: Rare and Unusual Perennials*. In 2003, Hinkley was honored with the Scott Arboretum Gold Medal from Swarthmore College in Pennsylvania for his lifetime achievements in horticulture.

JAMAICA KINCAID's books include *At the Bottom of the River, Annie John, A Small Place, The Autobiography of My Mother, My Brother, My Garden (Book)*, and *Mr. Potter*. She edited the anthology *My Favorite Plant* and is currently assembling a second such collection. She lives in Vermont.

ALLEN LACY is professor of philosophy emeritus at the Richard Stockton College of New Jersey. He was garden columnist for *The Wall Street Journal* for five years and for *The New York Times* for seven. His many books include *Home Ground, Gardening with Groundcovers and Vines, In a Green Shade*, and *The Inviting Garden*. With Nancy Goodwin he also wrote *A Year in Our Garden*, a book of letters between two gardening friends.

ABOUT
THE
CONTRIBUTORS

253

As photographers, writers, and plant historians, MICHELE and JEAN-CLAUDE LAMONTAGNE have devoted their professional lives to traveling the four corners of the globe in search of interesting gardens, unusual plants, and the relationship of both plants and gardens to human life. Separately and together, they have authored several books and contributed to many others and to magazines published throughout the world. They live in a small rural village near Paris.

CHRISTOPHER LLOYD is a hands-on gardener who has practiced all his life. Unlike most of the breed, he enjoys expressing himself in the written word and is a compulsive teacher. He has been writing books (including *The Well-Tempered Garden*) and articles for fifty years. His articles appear each week in *The Guardian* and *Country Life*. He frequently lectures and writes for publications in the United States.

TOVAH MARTIN acts as garden editor for *Victoria* magazine and the *Litchfield County Times*, and is the author of several gardening books. Her most recent titles include *A Time to Blossom: Mothers, Daughters, and Flowers*; *Garden Whimsy*; and *Heirloom Flowers*. She gardens extensively on the acres around her northwestern-Connecticut converted barn, but her heart belongs to the houseplants she first encountered when her horticultural career began, years ago, at Logee's Greenhouses.

JULIE MOIR MESSERVY is a landscape designer from Wellesley, Massachusetts. She is the author of three books, including the award-winning *The Inward Garden: Creating a Place of Beauty and Meaning*. Among her many private and institutional gardens, in collaboration with the eminent cellist Yo-Yo Ma, she designed the Toronto Music Garden, a three-acre public park, composed to the music of the First Suite for Unaccompanied Cello by J. S. Bach.

Former actor ANTHONY NOEL is a London-based garden designer, writer, author, and lecturer whose work regularly appears on both sides of the Atlantic. He has written two books, *Terra-Cotta* and *Great Little Gardens*, both published by Frances Lincoln. His gardening style has been described as "classical with a dash of theater," and his entire gardening career has been inspired by meeting Vita Sackville-West at Sissinghurst when he was nine years old.

MIRABEL OSLER has lived abroad in Thailand and Greece, and loves food and travel as well as roses. She gives talks on gardening, writes for magazines and newspapers, and is the author of books on restaurants, chefs, and markets in France. Her books include *A Gentle Plea for Chaos*, *The Secret Gardens of France*, *A Breath from Elsewhere*, *In the Eye of the Garden*, and *The Elusive Truffle*.

MICHAEL POLLAN is the author of *The Botany of Desire* and *Second Nature*, from which his essay on roses is adapted. He is also a contributing writer to *The New York Times*, and a contributing editor to *Harper's Magazine*. His garden is in Cornwall, Connecticut. However, he now lives at an unfortunate remove from it, in Berkeley, California, where he teaches in the Graduate School of Journalism.

ANNE RAVER is a garden columnist and environmental writer for *The New York Times*. An environmental educator, she enjoys giving talks about the adventure of gardening, and has taught in nature walks at a Maryland farm, garden programs in Brooklyn and Boston, and a children's farm in Beacon, New York. She is the recipient of numerous honors, including the Harvard Graduate School of Design's Loeb Fellowship in 1998 and the 2002 American Horticultural Society Writing Award, and is the author of *Deep in the Green*, a collection of essays about gardening, the natural world, family, and friends. She is currently at work on a new book.

PETER SCHNEIDER is editor of the *Combined Rose List*, the annual directory of roses in commerce (www.combinedroselist.com). He is the author of *Peter Schneider on Roses* and grows about twelve hundred different old and new roses in rural Ohio.

LAUREN SPRINGER is an American gardener, designer, and writer. She grew up on the Eastern Seaboard and has lived in northern Colorado for the past fourteen years. Her books include *The Undaunted Garden* (1994) and *Passionate Gardening* (2002). She designed the Watersmart, Fragrance, and Romantic Gardens at Denver Botanic Gardens.

PAMELA STAGG won The Royal Horticultural Society Gold Medal, the world's top prize for botanical painting, in 1991. Her work has been touring the world for more than five years in the Shirley Sherwood collection, and is represented in the Hunt Institute for Botanical Documentation in Pittsburgh, the world's leading public collection of botanical art. In addition to teaching, she has written a book about Toronto's SkyDome, and magazine articles on everything from wine to Canada's rare Spirit Bear.

For the last thirty years of his life, GRAHAM STUART THOMAS was considered the greatest living gardener in the world. Thomas's career spanned eight decades, and included distinguished accomplishments as a nurseryman, garden designer, botanical artist, garden historian, and memoirist. For many years, he was Garden Consultant to the National Trust. Thomas was the author of twenty books, most notably the *Graham Stuart Thomas Rose Book*, and on his ninetieth birthday, *The Garden Through the Year*. His last book, of reminiscences of famous gardeners he knew, is to be published in 2004.

DAVID WHEELER is the founder and editor of the British gardening quarterly *Hortus*, editor of *The Penguin Book of Garden Writing* (1996), and author of books about Cotswold gardens and the garden at Glyndebourne Opera in Sussex.

WAYNE WINTERROWD grew up in Shreveport, Louisiana, where he began gardening at the age of four. After a long career as a teacher of English literature, he devoted himself full-time to gardening and to writing about gardens. In 1977 he began, with Joe Eck, the creation of North Hill, their garden in southern Vermont.

CYNTHIA WOODYARD is a freelance photographer and garden designer based in Portland, Oregon. She has collaborated on several garden books, notably with Allen Lacy on *The Inviting Garden*, with Wayne Winterrowd on *Annuals for Connoisseurs*, and with Patrick Bowe on *The Complete Kitchen Garden*. Her photographs have appeared in many national and international magazines and publications.

INDEX OF ROSE NAMES